O9-AIE-490

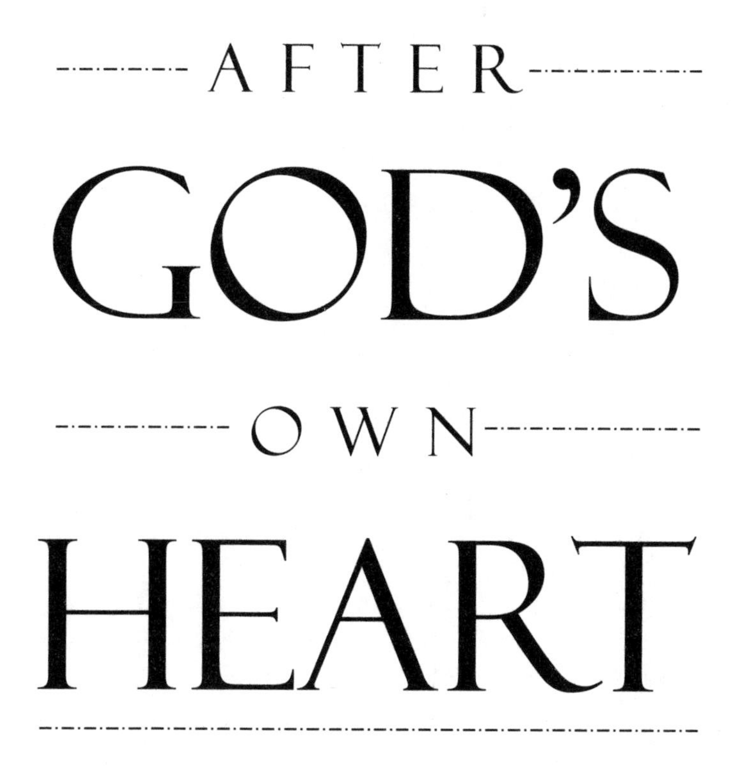

MIKE BICKLE

Charisma® HOUSE
A STRANG COMPANY

Most Strang Communications/Charisma House/Siloam products are available at special quantity discounts for bulk purchase for sales promotions, premiums, fund-raising, and educational needs. For details, write Strang Communications/Charisma House/Siloam, 600 Rinehart Road, Lake Mary, Florida 32746, or telephone (407) 333-0600.

After God's Own Heart by Mike Bickle
Published by Charisma House
A Strang Company
600 Rinehart Road
Lake Mary, Florida 32746
www.charismahouse.com

Cover design by Karen Grindley

Library of Congress Cataloging-in-Publication Data

Bickle, Mike.
After Gods own heart / Mike Bickle.
p. cm.
ISBN 1-59185-230-7 (Hardback)
1. Christian life—Biblical teaching. I. Title.
BS680.C47B53 2004
248.4—dc22

2003020968

04 05 06 07 08 — 9 8 7 6 5 4 3 2 1
Printed in the United States of America

DEDICATION

I want to dedicate this book to my dear son Paul, who just graduated from college and jumped into the IHOP-KC world. It is my joy to have you around so much. I love watching you receive and respond to God's Word. Wow! From the day you were born until your teen years, your mother and I laid hands on you literally every night while you lay sleeping in your bed. We asked the Lord to fill you with revelation of Jesus and to make you a man after His own heart. As I see you in these days, I am watching God answer these prayers right before my eyes. I cannot tell you how deeply this touches me. The Lord has surely called you to greatness before Him. May you see your destiny in the chapters of this book. You and Luke continue to be the delight of my heart.

DAD

ACKNOWLEDGMENTS

First, I want to thank my dear comrades Matt and Dana Candler for their invaluable help in taking my transcribed sermons and turning them into the manuscript for this book. The only way they were able to do this is because they live this message in their private lives.

I want to thank my friend and co-worker Bob Fraser for his relentless encouragement (pressure) to write this book. He refused all my good reasons for not having time to write another book.

I want to thank my personal assistant, Anne House, for tirelessly providing the transcriptions. Anne, you are a joy and blessing to so many at the International House of Prayer of Kansas City.

Thank you, Joel Kilpatrick, for the excellent work you did with the manuscript. You definitely improved it.

CONTENTS

FOREWORD

While playing in Kansas City in 1999, Delirious? had the pleasure of meeting Mike Bickle for the first time. We swapped "God" stories and immediately felt a connection with this radical man of God. We all left Kansas City that night with a greater sense of purpose, and so it is with great honor that I encourage you to read this book.

Holiness is always an awkward subject for today's generation of Christians. It's a word not often used these days, and let's be honest. It sounds a little bit boring!

I have often reflected on the true meaning of being a history maker. The more I carry on in my own Christian journey, the more I realize it is all to do with holiness, not the holiness that puts us in a straitjacket, but the holiness that celebrates purity and friendship and that jealously seeks after God's own heart. I have come to realize more and more that this holiness is not a "super-spiritual" set of rules that we all fall short of, but it is an everyday combination of good, godly choices and a passion to serve our Maker.

It's not about winning, but running... not about success, but commitment... not about position, but servanthood... not about religion, but relationship... not about liberalism, but discipline... not about compromise, but devotion. Holiness is happiness, and God is raising up a generation of revivalists whose heartbeat is to adore their heavenly Maker. Mike is the real deal and is someone who lives it, not just preaches it. Fasten your seat belts as you read, and prepare to be changed.

—Martin Smith
Delirious?

1

Chapter One

A GENERATION AFTER GOD'S OWN HEART

King David has been a puzzle, a mystery, a holy conundrum for thousands of years. His life perplexes, maddens, and humbles students of the Bible. To many, it doesn't make sense that this man who was so prone to personal weakness was able to "get away with" so much and still have God treat him with special favor. He was many things: a shepherd, a psalmist, a king, a liar, a murderer, and an adulterer. But most important of all, he was the only person in the entire span of the Bible to be called a man after God's own heart. Can you think of four more stunning words in all of creation? A man—lowly and often full of doubts and sin, like all of us—and yet God singled him out and called him a man after His own heart. What an awesome, almost unfathomable compliment!

But in saying those words, God threw open the door to every person on the planet to be, like David, a man or woman after God's own heart. We all have the same opportunity as that long-ago king to embody in our own personality and in our own way the kind of heart that reflects the very heart, emotions, and personality of God. Our Father is no respecter of persons. He didn't make King David great so the rest of us would feel like failures. Rather, He offers you and me the same opportunities and blessings He offered to men and women throughout history. But most people don't ever come close to having a heart after God's the way David did. They stumble and struggle through life without discovering God's heart and without letting it transform them.

> WHAT SET DAVID APART AS A MAN AFTER GOD'S HEART WAS HIS UNRELENTING PASSION TO SEARCH OUT AND UNDERSTAND THE EMOTIONS OF GOD.

One of the toughest questions throughout Christian history has been, "Why did David get this special distinction from God? What set him apart from so many other godly men and women?" In these days, I believe God is releasing the answer to that question in greater measure than ever before. You see, it wasn't David's obedience that earned him special standing with God. Close examination reveals he wasn't any more obedient than, say, Moses or the other prophets. And if you really want a sterling example of obedience, check out Daniel.

It wasn't David's pursuit of God's miraculous power that made him unique. Elijah and Elisha had many more power demonstrations.

And it wasn't his brilliant military success. That too wasn't one of a kind. Joshua had significant success in his military career, but he wasn't called a man after God's heart.

So, what made David the one person God called the man after

His own heart? What can we learn from him? What distinctive quality of his can we emulate as we seek to become men and women after God's heart?

The answer has the power to revolutionize the way you see God, the way you relate to Him, how you view yourself and your destiny in Him. What set David apart as a man after God's heart was his unrelenting passion to search out and understand the emotions of God. This, I believe, is the distinguishing factor in the life of any person—you or me or anyone else—who sets out to have a heart after God's. In fact, someday the church worldwide will be like David in this regard. We will be a massive group of people who worship, serve, and love God with ever-increasing understanding of His emotions and passions. Like David, we will understand and reflect the heart of God in a way humanity has rarely seen.

I believe we live in the generation in which the Lord will return, the generation that God will look upon and say, "They are after My own heart." Today, as in David's day, He seeks lovesick worshipers who understand how He feels. Jesus said, "But the hour is coming, and now is, when the true worshipers will worship the Father in spirit and truth; for the Father is seeking such to worship Him" (John 4:23). To worship in spirit is to worship deeply from a heart of total abandonment. Compare that to the limited way most people worship, staying within the strictures of external forms and religious rituals. True worship is not often seen on the earth. To worship, serve, and love the real way—God's way—demands something more than what we usually see on Sunday mornings or Wednesday evenings. To worship in truth means more than just singing the right songs or striking the right worship poses; it means understanding the truth about God's heart and personality. Worship is not a twenty-minute period during a church service but a lifestyle of relating to God in a particular way. But if you look at the body of Christ today, you see that religion has burdened us with lies about God's heart; it has hindered us from giving God the "love responses" we naturally desire to give Him. The turbulent rivers of affection in God's personality flow strong, and yet we respond with the drip-drip of ritual or passionless worship. When Jesus said, in John 4:23, that God was seeking for worshipers, He was referring to the tremendous, fierce, fiery desire in His Father's heart. That love seeks out lovers to requite His passion, to understand His love, and to worship Him drenched in the desire He has for us. That's what it means to be a true worshiper. David was such a man. And we must be men and women like him.

In this book we will look at David's life, which is a divine pattern for the church at the end of the age. It sets the course for our journey into holy passion and abandonment that will change our hearts in ways we haven't yet imagined and that will strengthen and empower the church in a way history has never seen. Millions of people are primed and ready for this change. Many are already on the path toward discovering God's own heart. Perhaps you are one of them, or perhaps you are hearing this for the first time, and your heart is burning inside of you at the possibility of becoming what you know the Lord wants you to be. Let me encourage you: you can be a person after God's own heart, just as David was. God is raising believers up and giving them hearts like David's. We will be, when all is said and done, a church after God's own heart. Let's start the journey into how.

After God's Own Heart

What does it mean to be a man or a woman after God's own heart? What in the heart of this shepherd boy playing his makeshift guitar on the backside of Bethlehem so captured almighty God's attention? I've alluded to one answer, but there are three facets to this divine description of David's life, and they form the basic blueprint for this book.

1. David was committed to obeying the commands of God's heart.

I put this first not because it's the most important, but because it's the most common, most recognizable lesson preachers draw from David's life. I have heard many men and women teach on this through the years, saying it's the key to being a person after God's heart, and while partly true, it's not the whole story. David's obedience is well established in the Book of Psalms and elsewhere. But it's only one dimension of what it means to be people after God's heart. We must look deeper.

Let's not deceive ourselves: it's critically important to obey God. Jesus equated obedience with love (John 14:23). David was tenacious, determined, and sincerely devoted to following hard after God's commands. This desire chiseled and shaped his heart over many years. But he was far from a model of obedience. There was often a yawning gap between his sincere resolve and his actions. In other words, he blew it from time to time, sometimes in spades. Yet he was still a man after God's own heart. That should flutter your heart a bit! What does this tell us? That there's more to being a person after God's heart than obedience. There is also the posture of your heart before God. God counted the sincere intentions of David's heart even when his great weakness led him to wrong decisions.

> THAT LOVE SEEKS OUT LOVERS TO REQUITE HIS PASSION, TO UNDERSTAND HIS LOVE, AND TO WORSHIP HIM DRENCHED IN THE DESIRE HE HAS FOR US.

God sees us the same way. *Our sincere intentions to obey are very significant to God.* He notices our desires, not just our outward actions. We often think that if our genuine intentions don't immediately come into full fruition, they are worthless. Religious tradition has taught us that only mature love for God is real love. It says when our love is immature, it's false and hypocritical. It blames young believers for messing up.

That's a damaging lie that strips people of confidence and dignity. Truth be told, we all start with immature love. Life is long because maturity takes time—often more time than we would like. Have you noticed that nobody immediately goes to heaven after accepting Jesus? Maturity requires time to develop, but sincere love of any maturity is real in God's eyes. It counts! God did not view David as a hypocrite while David's love was weak and immature, and He doesn't see us as hypocrites, either. Our attainment of mature love happens over months, years, and decades, and the results will be seen in due time as we bear fruit. God, in His patience, sees the long view much better than we do.

Most people beat themselves up over their weaknesses, but David saw God's heart more clearly than most of God's Old Testament servants and most Christians today. He understood that his deep-down determination to obey and love was valued by God, even when he came up short. David's weaknesses were at times paraded before his countrymen, even written into Scripture. Yet he had an unusual ability to stand confidently before God and say, "I am one of Your favorites. You like me even in my down times. I am completely Yours." This sincere determination to love Jesus even in the midst of our weakness is a huge part of being a man or woman after God's own heart. Our ability to obey will grow over time, but God doesn't treat us according to our obedience alone.

2. David was a student of God's emotions.

David went beyond a determination to sincerely obey; he became a student of God's emotions. He wanted to know what wonders, pleasures, and fearsome things filled God's heart. He had many responsibilities and challenges as warrior and king, but he spent his best energies trying to understand what emotions burned in the personality of God. This was a king like no other; he spent his days gazing upon the beauty of God's fiery desires and peering into the heart of the Uncreated One. It is this reality, not some legalistic impulse, that fueled David's obedience. He had a remarkable hunger to understand the emotions and heart of God, and as a result he had a unique grasp of the emotions, intentions, and passions of God's heart. David was, bar none, the Old Testament's ultimate student of the emotions of God. He was a scholar of God's affections; his bread and butter was an undying passion for the center flame of God's heart.

> OUR ATTAINMENT OF MATURE LOVE HAPPENS OVER MONTHS, YEARS, AND DECADES, AND THE RESULTS WILL BE SEEN IN DUE TIME AS WE BEAR FRUIT.

This is the one key, the single motivation that empowered David. And if we are to follow in his footsteps toward an understanding of God's heart, we must have the same motivation. By the anointing and the grace of God, we must become scholars of God's heart. We must yearn to know how God feels, how the passions of His heart move. *As we discover the same truths about God's heart, we will find ourselves living the way David lived and fulfilling the call of God on our generation.*

The Holy Spirit is impressing this upon people across the earth. He is taking what David saw in the heart of God, combining it with all that Jesus revealed about the Father's heart in the New Testament, and causing an explosion of revelation about the emotions of God's heart to come into the body of Christ. People are listening to this message and developing rock-solid resolve to be scholars of God's emotions, as David was. This explains the deep, worldwide hunger people have to experience God in a way that goes beyond what many churches are accustomed to. We will talk more about that later. For now we must fix it in mind that David was a man after God's heart primarily because he sought to understand the emotions of God—and we must do the same.

3. David was passionate about seeing the full release of the power and promises of God in his generation.

David refused to live with less than the very highest God would give him in his day. He never let himself feel disqualified by his weaknesses, but he contended mightily for the release of God's power during his generation. He caught a glimpse of God's zeal for His people and became convinced that the Lord would release His power for the benefit of the entire nation of Israel. In David's generation, God's power was often expressed in military feats. Therefore, entering into all that God would give his generation translated into military conquest of enemies. The principle today is the same, though not expressed in military terms. But like David, we must refuse to draw back until we experience God's full power for our generation. When we get caught up in the glorious emotions that burn within God's heart as David did, we begin to see the tremendous, unprecedented blessing and power God has planned for this hour in history. We lose our ability to settle for same ol', same ol'. We burn like torches with strong vision as our fuel. We become people who contend for the power of God available to our generation.

THIS JOURNEY TO BEING A PERSON AFTER GOD'S OWN HEART BEGINS WITH A REVELATION INTO THE EMOTIONAL MAKEUP OF THE HEART OF GOD.

To sum it up, let me switch the order to show the real sequence of how we become people after God's heart. David first passionately pursued the revelation of the desires and emotions of God's heart. Second, he obeyed God's commands, and third, he moved into the fullness of God's power and purposes. We'll dive into these critically important topics in later chapters.

This journey to being a person after God's own heart begins with a revelation into the emotional makeup of the heart of God. That is the first, most life-changing step, and there is no way around it. David conveyed what he saw in God's heart in dozens of ways through the songs and prayers he wrote. He prayed that he would be able to drink from the river of the pleasures of God's heart (Ps. 36:8). God's heart was depicted as a river, even a raging, crashing river of rushing desire for human beings. David understood that God's heart is like whitewater rapids, tossing and tumbling with fierce emotions so strong and determined that they even drove Him to the extreme of being incarnated and hung on a cross. In His love for us, He would simply not be denied relationship with us, and so He pursued us to the very end. *That* is the God we serve.

As you fix this picture of God in your mind, you will find your obedience is supercharged. You will mature much more rapidly than if you had plodded along with false views of a passionless God. You will go after the fullness of God's heart with astonishing energy as you are motivated from within by this revelation of His affections and desires for you. But you must intentionally pursue the revelation of God's heart and emotions to get the benefits. There is nothing passive about it. It's an aggressive hunt that requires as much energy and mental focus as any Olympic event. Remember, the main characteristic of a person after God's heart is that he or she understands and pursues the passion of God's heart for us—even in his or her weakness. The point is to keep going after knowledge of God's heart through all seasons of life. God invites us to pursue Him with abandon, and pursue we must if we are to have the incomparable pleasure of discovering Him.

Let's unlock this first, unique secret of David's life and see how he insisted on knowing the emotional heart of God.

The Pleasure of Encountering God

In the spring of 1999, I had a family meeting with my two sons, Luke and Paul, who were eighteen and twenty at the time. After being a pastor for twenty-five years, I was resigning the pastorate to lead the new International House of Prayer in Kansas City, Missouri, as my new full-time "job." Before announcing this publicly, I sat them down and told them I was leaving my salary, signing off the church board, and leaving that part of my life behind.

They looked at me with real surprise on their countenances. "Really?" they said.

I answered, "Yes, that is what I am going to do. I will soon resign from the church." They asked what I was going to do. I said, "Well, a group of worship leaders, intercessors, and myself are going to rent a little trailer and worship and pray there for hours a day."

My son said, "Great, Dad, but I mean, what will you do for your real job?" I assured them that this little trailer idea would eventually grow and other people would join us. Still perplexed, my sons looked at me as if to say, "OK, let me get this straight. You have no salary. You're going to rent a little trailer and put a couple of guitar players in it and sing and pray all day?"

I said, "So, what do you guys think?"

My boys love me a lot, so they said, "Good. OK, Dad. Whatever you say." One of them had the boldness to look at me sideways and ask, "Why?"

I told him, "I want to fast more, pray more, and worship more to release the Great Harvest. This may surprise you, but one reason I'm doing this is because I love pleasure."

They said, "Because you love pleasure?"

I said, "All the young guys you hang out with don't even compare to me. I have a much greater appetite for pleasure than they do. I'm addicted to wanting to feel more of God's presence. I must have more, and I must feel it deeper. I am a total pleasure addict. That's one reason I'm going to rent that trailer, get a couple of guitar players, fast, pray, worship, and study what Scripture says about the emotions of God."

I'm not sure they understood then, but I did. I had a vision in mind, learned from years of study and experience with God, and I was going to pursue it more aggressively than ever before. I had discovered that intimacy with God starts with the realization that *God likes us and wants to enjoy with us the pleasure of spiritual encounters with Him.* There is nothing more exhilarating for us than plunging into that river of pleasure. The glory of our lives is not just the fact that our generation will experience a revival that will surpass even the Book of Acts. That's great, and I'm happy to be part of it, but we are called to something even more profound: the infinite God of glory is truly in love with us, even in our weakness and brokenness. He has invited us to drink from the awesome spiritual pleasures of having a divine romance with Him. I don't know about you, but the best moments in my life are when God says to me, "I really enjoy you, Mike."

I DON'T KNOW ABOUT YOU, BUT THE BEST MOMENTS IN MY LIFE ARE WHEN GOD SAYS TO ME, "I REALLY ENJOY YOU, MIKE."

Enough said! I'm lost in that. I can't recover. I will never get over that message. I say back to Him, "God, there are one billion galaxies You made, and angels without number do Your bidding. The earth teems with life You created in almost infinite variety. These manifestations of Your glory are wonderful, but tell me again about the part I especially like: that You really like *me*." That's my favorite part of the whole gospel—when God says, "I really like you, Mike. Let's hang around together."

I don't think it's possible to outgrow the thrill, the wonder, the overwhelming certainty of being loved and enjoyed. It is the single experience all humans grope for and cling to in human relationships and with God. Knowing you are loved by another person fills your days with endless marvels, no matter what's going on outside your heart. You go through problems as if they're cotton candy. Your car breaks down and you think, *Big deal*, because somebody loves you. You lose your wallet, get caught in traffic, and forget the milk in the trunk all in the same day, but you don't even care because in your heart is that lamp lit with the strong power of love. You know that, should all else fail, you have this most important thing. God created us to be this way. He put deep longings to be loved inside of us. We were designed down to our DNA to live in spiritual pleasure of being enjoyed not just by other humans but also by Him.

GOD IS NOT A BORING FUDDY-DUDDY WHO WEARS SLIPPERS AND PUTTERS AROUND HEAVEN FEELING CONSTANTLY PERTURBED.

I'm not just talking about knowing in your head that God loves you. Everybody knows that, or says they do. But we've been numbed over the ages to the impact of God's love. We have reduced it to something namby-pamby and full of condescension and pity. Yet God's love is so full of tumbling energy and strong emotion, I don't know if we would recognize it for what it is. It is a wonderful thing to be loved, but I'm talking about actually feeling this transcendent love. They are two different things. One is knowledge, the other experience. One you might say to your spouse on your way out the door; the other you say to him or her in the bedroom, face to face, knee to knee, breath to breath. Mere knowledge of love makes life a little more bearable in the midst of the world's madness, but feeling love turns life into an utterly pleasurable adventure.

Most believers are so disconnected from the reality of God's astonishing, frightfully lavish love for us that they totally miss out on 99 percent of what they could experience in their everyday walk with Christ. They treat God like an employer, a business partner, a judge, a traffic cop—anything but a lover. They rarely feel His passion, love, or pleasure. Perhaps they tell themselves that feeling it is not all that important, as long as they are obeying His commands, reading the Bible, and keeping up the spiritual disciplines. But as a consequence of this dryness, they rarely feel love or pleasure of any kind.

You have to understand: God is not a boring fuddy-duddy who wears slippers and putters around heaven feeling constantly perturbed. He is not geriatric, but ageless. He is the very fountain of timeless youth and passion. He is the source of all pleasure in the universe! Happiness comes from no other source. It is *never* a sacrifice to hang out in His presence, though many are bored during times of prayer and worship. Most believers put prayer in the "sacrifices-I-make-for-God" category, but that only happens when you live with a total misconception of who God is. When we look into His heart, He reveals to us what He looks like emotionally and what we look like to Him. The result turns our brains and hearts inside out. You can't get over it! It's like falling in love for the first time. *He absolutely burns with love for you!*

> "Let not the wise man glory in his wisdom, let not the mighty man glory in his might, nor let the rich man glory in his riches; but let him who glories glory in this, that he understands and knows Me, that I am the LORD, exercising lovingkindness, judgment, and righteousness in the earth. For in these I delight," says the LORD.
>
> —JEREMIAH 9:23–24

In this passage God talks about people who relate to Him in wrong ways, usually based on their own attainment, rather than relating to Him based on His heart. It says in verse 23, "Let not the wise man glory in his wisdom." The wise man may be the scientist, the great inventor, or the theologian with biblical knowledge. The Lord urges him not to find confidence in what he knows. He then says, "Don't let the mighty man glory in his might." This could be a CEO or the president of a nation. The ability to move armies or great amounts of money or resources is not something to glory in.

Next God addresses the rich man: "Do not let the rich man have confidence in how much he has earned or accumulated. His riches will not secure him." Rather, He says, "Let the one who has confidence have confidence in this, that he understands Me. He knows My heart, that I delight in exercising lovingkindness." We are to glory in the fact that God is tender and kind when He relates to weak people. He is gentle with us in our weakness and filled with love for us even before we are spiritually mature.

As we will see, there is no greater testimony in Scripture of someone so weak and yet so great in God than that of David. He spent much time pondering and meditating on the emotions of God. He gloried in God's kindness, not in his own spiritual attainment. That is the opposite of how so many believers live! They don't put confidence in God's mercy and love, so they make life into a hard, cold, demanding thing, devoid of pleasure. They cut off the source of love and quietly put confidence in their own attainment. When they fail somehow, the self-blame is almost too much to bear. Beloved, that is the opposite of what it means to be a person after God's heart. Yes, there were times when David's confidence wavered, but the rule of his life, through its many seasons, was the certainty of who he was before God. That certainty must grow to dominate our hearts if we are to fulfill our generation's mandate.

God then said, "Let him be confident that I am a God who exercises judgment and righteousness. And in these I delight." Even when God judges, He is revealing His heart to remove things that hinder love. He will not be a silent witness or a distant observer. Passivity and isolation are not in His character. He insists on being an active, passionate participant in our lives. He will intervene with judgment when things stand in the way of the tender kiss of intimacy we can have with Him. He won't allow the relationships He treasures to be disrupted. He is a God of righteousness, and He desires not just to forgive us a billion times over, but to *change us into His very own likeness by inviting us into intimate relationship with Him.*

The Crisis: A False View of God

Imagine this great tragedy: A woman walks with God for forty years, fully saved, redeemed, and following Christ. She comes before the throne in the resurrection, and for the first time, she realizes what she's missed. She feels wave upon wave of pleasure flowing from the Son of God, and she says to herself, "I could have drunk from this well of spiritual delight every day on earth. I just had to encounter Your heart and Your beauty. Life would have been so much better! Everything would have changed, and I would have accomplished so much more." Many like her spend their days on earth believing that Jesus is harsh instead of tender, mad instead of glad, and distant instead of affectionate. When they finally see Him as He truly is, they will be filled with regret at not spending their time on Earth radically pursuing His heart and reaping the amazing pleasures.

Beloved, we don't have to wait to experience the deep pleasures! God has ordained for the human heart to experience them *even in this life.* I'll go further and state that it's not optional for us to go on as generations have, without a transforming revelation of God's heart. In light of the mounting pressures at the end of the age, we can't afford to *not* drink of the pleasures of His heart. Our lives must overflow with constant delighted cries of, "O God, this is too good to be true; it's too magnificent to really be happening! But it is true! Beyond what I could hope for!" We want these testimonies of worship and adoration to flow from our spirits now and not just in eternity. We desperately need hearts anchored and sustained by an outrageous love that comes from another world.

BELOVED, YOU AND I CANNOT PRODUCE A GOOD ENOUGH ARGUMENT TO CHANGE GOD'S EMOTIONS TOWARD US!

The present crisis in the body of Christ, in which many people never experience the love of God, stems from a false view of God. Instead of a God who is full of tenderness, gladness, and desire, believers imagine a God who is filled with animosity toward them. This affects every single aspect of how they approach Him.

Think of it in practical terms. When you are forced to meet with someone who openly dislikes you, considers you a hypocrite, or is full of blame toward you, your spirit is guarded and closed. You can't relax. You count the minutes and look forward to leaving that person's presence. This is how many of God's people live and worship. They lift hands and voices with guarded spirits and closed hearts. This is an amazing and sad statement, but most believers I know are trying to live a devoted life of holiness while seeing God as harsh and menacing. They are unable to worship Him with open spirits because inside they feel rejected by Him as a hopeless hypocrite. They may use different words to describe this reality, but the pain is the same. Perhaps you have felt it. You may sing, dance, speak in tongues, and pray for others, but you do it with your heart gate latched shut and a sign that reads "Do not disturb" hung on your spirit. You come before God as you would come before someone who despises you.

This common view of God produces churches full of believers who feel condemned. They are like mules lugging around huge loads of condemnation on their backs. They see themselves as prisoners on spiritual probation, and they try so hard to get their acts together. Even when they worship they silently negotiate with God, "Give me one more chance, and I promise I will never ask for anything else again. Forgive me one more time, and I will never again sin the way I did before." They continuously try to create a loving motivation in God's heart. Beloved, you and I cannot produce a good enough argument to change God's emotions toward us! His emotions are set and will not be altered. It's foolish to think we can cause Him to love us, but that's how many live—on the "wrong" side of God's emotions.

There is a cure for this, but first we must get real about the state of the body of Christ. Across the world today, many of God's people live in spiritual compromise. This is no secret to anyone who looks with honesty at the condition of the church. This crisis of backsliding stems from this false view of God's heart. But into this darkness, the Lord sends His words through the prophet Jeremiah:

> "Return, O backsliding children," says the LORD; "for I am married to you.... I will give you shepherds according to My heart, who will feed you with knowledge and understanding."
>
> —JEREMIAH 3:14–15

What is God going to do to correct the backsliding? Beat everyone up? Bring another Great Depression? Cause countries to suffer surprise military attacks? Spread incurable diseases? No, Jeremiah prophesied that in the End Times, God would cause His people to return wholeheartedly by revealing our relationship to Him as a cherished bride. This heart-stopping truth will be enough to prod the church out of lethargy. The Lord will cry out through His prophets, saying these profound words, "Return... for I am married to you."

This is the Lord's highest way of empowering people to walk in wholehearted holiness with Jesus. He doesn't whale on us with a switch from the willow tree, but He introduces us to our marriage relationship with the Godhead. He invites us to fill our spirits with the understanding of Him as our Husband, the One who is merciful, glad-hearted, affectionate, and beautiful. He beckons us to go on a journey that we might experience the power of this reality in our own being. And then, flowing out of our personal encounter with Him, we will stop our backsliding, proclaim what He is like to others, and lead them into their own experience of this fascinating, intimacy-loving Bridegroom God.

God's Promise: Shepherds After God's Own Heart

After God gives a beckoning call to return to Him because He is married to us, inviting us to come near to Him in confident love and wholeheartedness, He then gives a promise:

> I will give you shepherds according to My heart, who will feed you with knowledge and understanding.
>
> —JEREMIAH 3:15

In effect, He says, "I am going to raise up men and women who will experience the spiritual reality of God's heart as a Bridegroom God. That revelation will flow like a river on the inside of those shepherds, and they will live in the mighty power of this revelation. Then they will feed the church from it." The Lord is now raising up men and women after His heart, like David, and He will give them as a gift to the backslidden church to win her back to wholeheartedness. Watch and listen carefully so you can see the day coming.

The Lord also promised to give the End-Time church shepherds according to His own heart—men and women, old and young, who will give expression to this reality of a Bridegroom God for His people. It will happen soon. He declared that He would raise up servants who will speak this good news to the compromising people of God. They will speak it with deep, undeniable revelation and feed the people with the knowledge of God's heart. Their mandate will be to equip the people of God to understand what it means to be married to God. Daniel prophesied this when he said, "And those of the people who understand [God's heart] shall instruct many" (Dan. 11:33).

When Jeremiah prophesied that God was going to raise up shepherds after His own heart, it was approximately 600 B.C. The Lord borrowed a phrase that He Himself originally spoke over a young guitar player in the back hills of Bethlehem about four hundred years earlier. God spoke to Samuel, saying that David was a man after His own heart (1 Sam. 13:14). David was called this by God, not by the prophet. Samuel delivered the mail, but the message was from the Lord Himself, and it said, "This guy's heart is like Mine. I'm going to use him greatly."

Approximately four hundred years later, God echoed His earlier declaration over David by saying to the prophet Jeremiah, "I will raise up people in the End Times like David, people who will also be shepherds after My own heart. This will be fulfilled in the lives of multitudes of shepherds across the nations of the earth."

For us, that means that David's heart was not confined to him alone. Rather, he was a living prophecy of the Holy Spirit to the shepherds in the generation in which Jesus returns. This reality will spread further and deeper at the end of the age than at any time in history because He is going to reveal Himself as a Bridegroom. Not even David understood himself as the bride of Jesus. Based on what is recorded in Scripture, the first prophet to speak the message of the bride of Christ was Hosea about 750 B.C., around two hundred fifty years after David. That means we have a revelation that goes beyond what David saw in the heart of God. The shepherds in the End Times will have the same character of David's heart but with further understanding of the Bridegroom God.

This is what the Lord is doing in this hour of history. The Holy Spirit is raising up shepherds to teach God's people to live after His own heart. They will feed others from the reality they encounter through their own unyielding personal pursuit of God. They will only be able to shepherd others because they have given themselves wholly to the great Shepherd. Some of these shepherds will lead through preaching and some through writing, singing, or other skills and talents. Some will do it through one-on-one discipleship and spending time nurturing younger believers' faith in a spiritual relationship. Some will do it in the context of their business or workplace. Perhaps you are called to be a shepherd, to aggressively pursue the knowledge of His personality in your own life so you can feed others with the truths you discover. I encourage you to pray specifically about this. You can't afford to miss your appointment in these End Times.

As individual believers, we stand in two positions in regard to God's invitation to us. We first must feed our own spirits on the truths of this Bridegroom God's heart and personality, and then we will arise as shepherds in the body of Christ to feed others. We can't feed others if we don't feed ourselves first. Therefore we must become people with a clear focus on personally discovering who Jesus is in all of these dimensions of His Bridegroom heart. This includes giving time and energy to understanding this new paradigm of God. At some point in this process we will be equipped to lead other believers who are entrenched in compromise. We'll take them by the hand and show them into the freeing and empowering encounter of what our God is like. It's not enough to tell people that God is a Bridegroom and we are His bride. It must come from our hearts. It is transformation by personal revelation. This revelation has to be "unpacked" and broken down into bite-size pieces. Shepherds must unfold specific elements of God's emotions that have been wrongly taught from the Word of God. They will train people and feed them on specific parts of God's emotions and personality, and then, little by little, like a flower in spring, the listeners' spirits will open up and be transformed.

THE HOLY SPIRIT IS RAISING UP SHEPHERDS TO TEACH GOD'S PEOPLE TO LIVE AFTER HIS OWN HEART.

In raising up multitudes of shepherds, God is doing the same type of thing He did in David's day. Back then there was no widespread revelation in the land (1 Sam. 3:1). So what did the Lord do? He put His hand on a young shepherd boy with revelation of His heart. What a great gift to that land! And the shepherds of today are likewise a gift to the body of Christ. The Lord says, "I have not forgotten My people. I am raising up young men and women, and I will touch them with the same anointing of revelation of My heart, just as I touched David. They will slay the Goliaths of their day the same way David did, by understanding My heart."

God will bring this same heart of David, plus the bridal paradigm, into fruition in multitudes of weak and broken human beings in the generation that the Lord returns. Beloved, this is about us! We have been invited into the revelation that David experienced. You can be one of those who walk in the heart of God and fulfill those astonishing four words, being a man or woman "after God's own heart"!

David's life should embolden you to say, "Why not me? If he can overcome his failure and still have confidence in God's tender mercy, then I can!"

There is no doubt: the church at the end of the age will be a church after God's own heart. It's a done deal. God gave us the life of David not to fill us with awe but to change our thinking, to get us ready. David was a man like us, weak and with spiritual failures. But he succeeded before God in his spiritual life. A thousand years after David died, God even did some wonderful editing of David's legacy. The apostle Paul said, "He [God] raised up for them David as king... and said, 'I have found David the son of Jesse, a man after My own heart, who will do all My will'" (Acts 13:22). I love God's editing process. A thousand years after David died, Paul declared that David did, in fact, do all God's will. What about all the failures and setbacks? Edited out by the grace of God. He will do that in your life, too, if you have His heart.

David's life should embolden you to say, "Why not me? If he can overcome his failure and still have confidence in God's tender mercy, then I can!" Real man or woman of God, real Bible heroes were just like you and me. Weak-kneed, unfaithful, puny—but before the throne of God they are counted a success. And we will be, too.

This generation bears the singular distinction of having *unprecedented revelation* into God's emotions. Because of this we will do what no other generation has done. We will enter into an understanding and a profound transformation of beholding the wonders of God's heart.

How does the Lord bring an entire generation of believers into this great anointing that David lived in? There are several important lessons we will go into in greater depth. I want to start with a new approach to a subject that formerly filled people with fear but that now will fill us with absolute joy. Really, it is the old approach that worship clearly established in the Word of God, but it is new to some in this generation. I'm talking about holiness—or rather, holy obsession that God is raising up in the body of Christ to replace the dreary rituals of sacrifice. I think you will be surprised at the direction of the next chapter.

Chapter Two

FROM RELIGIOUS SACRIFICE TO HOLY OBSESSION

Some years ago the Lord visited my spiritual father, Paul Cain, who is now in his mid-seventies and has been prophesying for more than sixty years. The Lord spoke to him and said that He was going to raise up a young adult movement all over the world and reveal to them a new approach to holiness. He spoke to Paul about something new in terms of our Christian traditions. It will not be new in terms of Scripture. It will be an approach to holiness that "wows" people with a revelation of His tenderness. Instead of being motivated by fear or shame, believers will be empowered to holiness because of the affection for us that burns in God's heart. The highest and best way of motivating the human heart to righteousness is through fascination and exhilaration in love. As the Lord told Paul Cain, He is raising up millions of sons and daughters who are motivated in this way and who motivate others by this new approach to holiness, which the prophet Jeremiah described as being "married to the Lord" (Jer. 3:14).

Secondary Motivating Forces

David knew what holiness was. He wrote, "Preserve my soul; for I am holy: O thou my God, save thy servant that trusteth in thee" (Ps. 86:2, KJV). All across the body of Christ and stretching back through all of Christian history, we find different methods people have used to motivate the human heart to turn to the Lord. Preachers and revivalists of many different persuasions have stroked various heartstrings to accomplish this. Some emphasized the fear of punishment, crying, "Return! For if you don't, you will face eternal damnation." Now don't get me wrong—this is a true and biblical motivation for repentance. People really will go to hell if they don't repent and make Jesus the Lord of their lives. The desire to escape eternal judgment is one of the powerful incentives God has given us to flee from darkness into light. The Bible describes people who respond to this motivating force as those snatched from the burning fire (Jude 23). In our day, some people joke that such converts are just getting fire insurance, but it's fire insurance that works. The terrors of hell awaken their hearts, and they return to the Lord. But fear of hell is not God's primary way of drawing the human heart toward Himself.

Another common tactic of holiness preaching is to promote *fear of missing out on revival.* You may have heard preachers say things like, "If you don't turn to the Lord, you will never operate in a greater anointing. Press in and pay the price so you can be part of the revival." Preachers like this urge people to go hard after God in order to be powerfully used by Him. In essence, they promote God as a means to an end: if we press into God, then we get the reward—revival. Revival is good and necessary, but it's not the best motivator. This urgency to be part of what God is doing works for some people for a short while, but over time it has little staying power. It usually inspires strong resolutions, symbolic actions, grandiose statements, many tears. But it typically dies out when the person crashes into his or her weakness, or when the thrill of the meetings ends.

You may have seen this happen to someone in your church. He sincerely wants to do more and be more for God, and upon hearing the sermon about pressing in and not missing revival, he repents from some sin that he has allowed in his life. Perhaps he enrolls in a Bible course or commits to attending every prayer meeting the church offers. But after a while, life happens. He fails somehow, slips into sin, or does something stupid. Doubts rise from the ashes of his failure and prevail over his initial resolve. Determination morphs into discouragement. Revival fades away, and there's no incentive to stick with his commitments, so he goes back to being the kind of believer he was before. Though this form of motivation to holiness is also biblical, it is still not the highest method God has for His people.

Other leaders in the body of Christ throughout history have motivated people through the *fear of shame.* They declare, "Turn from your ways, or you will get caught and be put to shame. If you sin, you will be exposed and humiliated before all." When you hear this motivation, a cold shiver goes down your spine. Oh, the pain of shame! Yet the initial impact usually dissipates after the cold shivers stop. You maneuver your way out of this motivation by imagining that you can beat the system and not get caught. You persuade yourself, with false confidence, that you will never really encounter the penalty. That's probably not true—there's always a penalty, and it's usually embarrassing to have your sin exposed—but the idea of shame, though biblical, has limited effect in our ability to truly live holy lives.

Our Highest Motivation: He Wants to Marry Us

God intimately understands the human heart, which He formed. He knows perfectly how to motivate His people toward holiness.

I have referenced Jeremiah 3:14, where the Lord says, "Return, O backsliding children...for I am married to you." This very revelation is the highest and most effective motivator for calling people to abandon all else for Him. Great desire for human beings is the secret weapon in God's arsenal. The power of this revelation when we grab on to it is simply unmatched by any other revelation in the universe. It is not built on shame or fear but on strong desire. He says in essence, "Turn to Me because I am married to you and because I desire you." He is not negating all of the other types of biblical motivation, but He is making it clear what the superior motivation is. This will become the single most important impulse toward holiness in the final hour of natural history as the Lord raises up a bride with a heart after God's.

Let me repeat, so no one misunderstands: The secondary forms of motivation are *valid*. Hell is a *true* reality. And we experience real loss in our spiritual lives and in the fullness of our earthly ministry by not fully responding to the Holy Spirit during revival. Shame and embarrassment lead to *genuine* pain when sin is exposed. All these arguments have their place. There is a time to warn people of hell or to warn them that they may lose out and be disqualified in terms of their earthly mandate and ministry. There is a time to exhort people to leave their ungodly ways because of the public and private humiliation they will taste if they don't. Yet the primary and most effective method is the way that the Lord Himself spoke through the prophet Jeremiah: "*Turn because I am married to you.* My heart burns with desire and longing for intimate fellowship with you. I yearn for close relationship and encounter between My heart and your heart." With this invitation, the Lord beckons us to do away with compromise and leave our backsliding *because He wants us and desires us*. The Lord is crying out "Return! Return!" to the backslidden children who have found their pleasures elsewhere. He is calling to the redeemed who have lost their way and whose hearts have grown cold. He is ready to "wow" them with a revelation of His heart that will cause true holiness to spring up like a geyser from within their spirits.

God has reserved this revelation for the generation in which His Son returns. This statement, "I am married to you," was rare in the Old Testament. Hosea spoke of it a little bit, and Isaiah touched on it a few times, but God only gave them whispers. There have been mere hints and adumbration of it throughout church history, and few preachers have focused on this spiritual reality for very long. And never in history has the company of the redeemed fully understood that they are the cherished bride. But in the last generation, the Holy Spirit will emphasize it with intensity. The knowledge that Jesus is a Bridegroom and we are His bride will crescendo and become a divine shout as we move toward the moment when the Spirit and the bride cry, "Come!" The Holy Spirit will emphasize the message of being married to the Lord with power in churches and gatherings of believers in every country. He will single out this message for its singular importance at this hour in time. As the message seizes the hearts of the hearers, the body of Christ will change dramatically in the way it approaches God. Church life, relationships, ministries, and outreaches will look different than they ever have. For the only time in history, the people of God across the earth will see themselves as a bride and Jesus as their eternal Bridegroom.

> GOD KNOWS PERFECTLY HOW TO MOTIVATE HIS PEOPLE TOWARD HOLINESS.

One of the greatest and most baffling truths about our eternal destiny is that God has ordained that He will share His heart with human beings. This bridal identity, this privileged position of intimate nearness to God's heart, far surpasses positions given to the angelic order and all the heavenly hosts. Our position is one of almost unimaginable spiritual privilege. The God of the universe opens His heart and shares the deep things of His being with us—that's more than staggering! I imagine an ancient boundary line that keeps the angels standing as servants at a distance from the heart of God. They are only allowed to approach to a certain point, and then they must stop. Yet the Lord Himself invites weak human beings to cross that ancient boundary line. He beckons us to come near. He gives to us what He keeps hidden from angels.

What does it mean to be married to the Lord? We begin by recognizing that He is a passionate Bridegroom. That leads us to understand that we are His prized bride. Our identity flows from Him. We cannot understand ourselves as a cherished bride until we know what our Husband is like. If we perceive God as angry and disappointed, how can we enter into our true identity? We'll have an inaccurate, distorted portrait of ourselves.

John the Baptist grasped this reality of the bride and Bridegroom. People peppered him with the same questions: "Who are you, and what are you about?" John answered by declaring who he was in light of the Bridegroom God.

> He who has the bride is the bridegroom; but the friend of the bridegroom, who stands and hears him, rejoices greatly because of the bridegroom's voice. Therefore this joy of mine is fulfilled.
>
> —John 3:29

John discovered who he was! He who has the bride is the Bridegroom. He was telling people they couldn't understand who he was apart from understanding Jesus as a Bridegroom.

Modern and "pop" psychology, which is pervasive in the world and even in the church, emphasizes self-discovery, or "discovering who I really am." This is an important thing to do, but it's out of sequence. The answer doesn't lie within yourself or your surroundings or your past. You will never discover "who you are" by examining your environment, your job, your family history, or the people you know. The secret to who you are lies in the heart of one Man alone. He is the Bridegroom God. Only by gazing in His eyes and understanding who *He* is will you know who *you* are. All other searching is in vain. How many hours, years, and lifetimes have been wasted as people gaze at their own hearts and come up empty? How many good people have fallen for theories and philosophies that put self-discovery at the top of the totem pole, only to leave them with no clue who they really are? The answer is in the other direction.

THE GOD OF THE UNIVERSE OPENS HIS HEART AND SHARES THE DEEP THINGS OF HIS BEING WITH US—THAT'S MORE THAN STAGGERING!

You shouldn't concern yourself at the beginning of the journey with finding out who you are. That will come in time. God will reveal you to you in a deeply meaningful, life-transforming way. But, like John the Baptist, you need to first discover who Jesus is as a Bridegroom and to feed your spirit on what His personality is like. When that knowledge begins to come alive in your mind and spirit, you will inevitably discover His affections, His desires, and His tender dealings with you in your weaknesses. You will see that you are indeed a cherished bride. The real you will emerge and blossom in light of who He is.

I have been preaching on the bride of Christ since 1988, and I regularly run into men who struggle to view themselves as the bride of Christ. They are troubled by the *female* description and think maybe we should just leave the bridal paradigm for women's ministry. But the position we stand in as the bride of

Christ is not about being male or female. Men are the bride of Christ just as women are the sons of God. Both identities describe a position of privilege that transcends gender. When the Bible calls men and women to be sons of God, it means He has given His authority to us. When God calls us the bride of Christ, it means He is sharing His heart in intimacy with us. In other words, the message of the bride of Christ is God inviting us to experience intimacy with the deep things of His heart.

THE SECRET TO WHO YOU ARE LIES IN THE HEART OF ONE MAN ALONE. HE IS THE BRIDEGROOM GOD.

> "Eye has not seen, nor ear heard, nor have entered into the heart of man the things which God has prepared for those who love Him." But God has revealed them to us through His Spirit. For the Spirit searches all things, yes, the deep things of God.
>
> —1 CORINTHIANS 2:9–10

The deep things of God's heart speak of His fiery emotions for us. The Holy Spirit desires to reveal these to us. This reality about God's heart is beyond anything that we have ever imagined. The fullness of this has not even entered the human heart. This is the way to live a fascinated life as a lovesick worshiper. Intimacy with God is not just an option, but it is the very essence of true Christianity.

Man of God, this message does not undermine your masculinity; it actually establishes it and gives you the only real way into full manhood. Consider how the Bible describes King David, John the Baptist, and the apostle John. These were *real men*. Each one would have been known in his day as a "man's man"; yet they were men who pressed into the privilege of experiencing the deep things of God's heart.

We get too hung up on the gender issue. Remember that King David was known as the great warrior king; however, he was the example of a lovesick worshiper of God. Was he any less a man? John the Baptist, the fiery prophet in the wilderness, referred to himself as a friend of the Bridegroom (John 3:29). Did that make him a sissy? The apostle John, the son of thunder, identified himself as the one that laid his head upon the Lord's breast (John 21:20). Did that sabotage his manhood? No. These men discovered the path to true intimacy, which is the privilege of both men and women in the body of Christ. Your position before God as the bride of Christ brings you into connection with the deep things of His heart. This is the truth of being married to the Lord, the greatest conceivable honor in the entire universe—for men and for women.

Bridegroom Foundation #1—the God of Tenderness

When we come before this passionate Bridegroom as His cherished bride, Jesus progressively reveals certain aspects of His heart to us. Typically, He begins with His tenderness and mercy. This is the same tenderness and mercy that encounter us at salvation, when we feel utterly weightless and free and jubilant—and rightly so. Jeremiah tells us God delights in showing us lovingkindness (Jer. 9:24). God knows we can bring nothing to the bargaining table to motivate Him to deal kindly with us. He is fully motivated within Himself to be merciful. But this is an extremely difficult message for people to receive. We are often too hard on ourselves, thinking that condemning ourselves will somehow make it all better or will help God to love us.

When sincere lovers of Christ stumble due to weakness or immaturity, they often hold it against themselves for months or even years. You may have met people who seem crippled by sins or tendencies, some of which are many years in the past. They may come to the altar repeatedly and weep and repent, though God forgave them years ago. The truth is, when we ask for forgiveness, the Lord forgives us instantly. His tenderness toward us far surpasses our own. We fashion our sins into a cat-o'-nine-tails and flay our backs, thinking this pleases God when all it does is grieve Him further. Oh, the tender dealings of the Bridegroom's heart! Oh, how great are His mercy, His lovingkindness, and His gentleness toward us!

The enemy works overtime against this revelation of God's mercy so we won't accept the full wonder of the Bridegroom's tenderness toward us. Mercy is the foundation of a powerful lifestyle that would rip Satan's kingdom to shreds. But most of the body of Christ is not established in even the most elementary understanding of God's mercy; millions of believers are trapped in a flat-out false view of God. They see Him as unreasonably fierce in His determination to get the job done, a demanding CEO, a hard-driving boss. They imagine He is bent on accomplishing His purposes without accepting mistakes along the way. They even imagine, in the dark corners of their minds, that He is willing to sacrifice a few of us if need be to complete the Great Commission. We would never say this aloud, but many people believe it. And so, when we blow it, mess up, or stumble, we respond to God as we would to an angry taskmaster. When we fumble the ball, we imagine He screams at us, kicks us off the team, and says, "How dare you fumble! We could have won that one!" We conclude that we are dispensable and disposable to God unless we perform perfectly.

GOD IS NEVER SURPRISED, DISILLUSIONED, OR CONFUSED BY OUR FAILINGS.

The only reason we are shocked when we stumble is because of our own religious pride. God is never surprised, disillusioned, or confused by our failings. I remember some occasions in my spiritual journey when I became almost numb after I made a mistake. One of those times, when I was about nineteen years old, I did something wrong and instantly prayed, "Lord, I can't believe I just did that!" The implication was, "God, I bet You can't believe it either." I was sure I had surprised God just as much as I had surprised myself. I pictured the look on His face, the sadness in His heart, the rising anger, the inevitable punishment I deserved. This kind of thing happened to Peter at the Last Supper in Matthew 26:31–35, when Jesus said, "All of you will stumble tonight." Peter slammed his hand down on the table and said, "Wait a minute! The other guys might, and You and I know they probably will, Lord. But one thing You can be sure of, I will never stumble. I will not deny You. Count on me!" Jesus corrected him, saying, "Peter, you will." But Peter, as foolish as we are, stuck to his guns and adamantly argued that he would go to his death before denying his Lord.

Like many of us, Peter had more confidence in his own dedication to the Lord than he had in the Lord's dedication to him. His relationship with Jesus was based on misplaced confidence in his own devotion. For this reason, Peter was probably the only one shocked when the rooster crowed and the sound of his third denial was still echoing off the walls. Though every believer's personal dedication to God is absolutely crucial, we must understand that our dedication to the Lord is only an outcome of His dedication to us.

The Lord says, "Then I will cause him to draw near, and he shall approach Me" (Jer. 30:21). It is the Lord who causes us to draw near to Him. The strength of our commitment and obedience is in the drawing power of Jesus' tender leadership. This is what Jesus wanted Peter to understand. I imagine Jesus saying, "Peter, when this thing is over, your confidence will be in what's in My heart, not what's in yours." And that's what He wants to teach us, too. God knew we would mess up. He saw it way in advance and made provision for it from the very beginning. David said, "For He knows our frame; He remembers that we are dust" (Ps. 103:14). He knows our frailty, both physical and emotional. He recognizes the limited capacity of our hearts. I say this not to make an excuse for compromise or to give license for sin, but to emphasize a God who recognizes and looks for our determination toward obedience over and above human frailty. He sees the *yes* in the hearts of His people and says, "I understand your weakness, and yet I recognize your willingness to be wholly Mine." He looks at the agreement in our hearts and calls forth our budding virtues into full maturity.

You see, we are dealing with a loving Bridegroom, the Man Christ Jesus. He is fully God, but He is also fully man. He has intense affections filled with tenderness. He doesn't wield a big hammer, hoping He can find good reason to smash us flat. Even while we grow and falter on our way to full maturity, He enjoys us, and His heart flows with extravagant compassion, the likes of which the world will never know without Him. Remember, the Lord said:

> Let not the wise man glory in his wisdom.... But let him who glories glory in this, that he understands and knows Me, that I am the LORD, exercising lovingkindness... in the earth. For in these I delight.
>
> —JEREMIAH 9:23–24

Few members of the body of Christ have been deeply impacted by this revelation. God is crying out for people to boast and have confidence in His lovingkindness. It neither pains nor frustrates Him to be kind. On the contrary, it gives Him pleasure. The prophet Micah declared what God requires of us: to do justly, *to love mercy*, and to walk humbly (Mic. 6:8). The Lord is saying, "I delight in mercy! I am at My best when I am showing mercy!"

This is the most fundamental idea to the Bridegroom God—He is a God of mercy toward you and me personally.

Bridegroom Foundation #2—the God of Gladness

The second revelation He gives us is that He is a God of gladness. I want to delve into this in more depth later, but I introduce it here because it's foundational to our understanding of the Bridegroom. Not only does He have unfathomable mercy, but also God possesses powerful pleasures beyond our comprehension. His rejoicing emotions are infinite in measure and eternal in duration. Experiencing God is like riding a roller coaster that never ends but gets better with each curve. He smiles with delight and enjoyment when He gazes on each one of us. This strikes many people as strange. They are accustomed to relating to a God who is mostly mad or mostly sad when they come before Him. They imagine that He is either mad because they have rebelled, or sad and grieved all the time because His people are not dedicated enough.

> HE SEES THE YES IN THE HEARTS OF HIS PEOPLE AND SAYS, "I UNDERSTAND YOUR WEAKNESS, AND YET I RECOGNIZE YOUR WILLINGNESS TO BE WHOLLY MINE."

In Luke 15:4–7, Jesus describes what God's emotions are like toward those who lose their way in weakness. He portrays the Father going after the lost sheep until He finds him. When He does, He lays him on His shoulders and carries him home, rejoicing with great gladness all the while. It's powerful enough to realize that God is not a distant, frustrated observer. But more powerful is knowing that when the Father finds us in the struggle of our weakness, in some shabby place of sin and self-loathing, He lifts us out of it with great enjoyment. What kind of God is this who actually enjoys us in the process of cleaning us up?

He is the God of gladness, a happy God of infinite joy. In the billions of years that we will relate to Him, His anger will only be for a brief moment, and the other 99.9999999 percent of our experience and relationship with Him will be based on the gladness of His heart toward us. He is a God of happy holiness, without any contradiction between those words. His holiness flows from abundant joy that cannot be imagined. This does not deny His anger with rebellion. He is fierce to remove what hinders the love between you and Him. But in the life of a sincere believer, there is an important distinction between rebellion and immaturity. They are entirely different things. God hates rebellion, but He sees immaturity as something than outright sin. He is smart enough to separate the individual from the sin. He can enjoy us and still disapprove of things we do or believe, like a parent who disciplines and enjoys a child from one moment to the next. That's how our Father is, and much more so.

THE GOD OF AFFECTION—THIS IS THE FOUNDATION TRUTH THAT YOU EXPERIENCE IN YOUR INTIMACY WITH JESUS.

Bridegroom Foundation #3—the God of Burning Desire

The third foundation is that our Bridegroom God burns with fiery affections. This fact is separate and distinct from His tenderness and great gladness. Most people have a hard time thinking of God as desiring or wanting anything. After all, He owns everything. His pantry is always stocked. He can create creatures and worlds and galaxies to bring Him pleasure. He could entertain Himself endlessly. But the fact is deeply rooted in Scripture that He is also full of intense desire and burning love for each of us. He longs to be near each one of us personally, in the way friends and lovers want to be together. This God of affection is what so many are longing to encounter, even though they may not be aware that the encounter will radically transform their heart.

The God of affection—this is the foundation truth that you experience in your intimacy with Jesus. This is what makes you great. This is what makes you special and unique in all the universe. This provides each of us with the primary definition for our lives.

Our success and value are not based on our level of production, our financial worth, our talent in sports, music, or academics, or anything else. These are all sideshows. What gives us true meaning in the vast, complex world in which we find ourselves is that the eternal One, the uncreated God, pursues us with passionate desire. This is what crowns our lives with meaning and power. This is what makes us great. We did nothing to become born, and since then we have stumbled and fallen in so many ways. Yet Jesus, our Bridegroom God, says, "I want you!" And that confers upon us eternal significance. We are the ones God desires. Though every other circumstance be unstable, and though we mess up in myriad ways, we walk in grace before an audience of One with profound success and contentment simply because He longs for us and declares Himself the lover of our souls. The church in a bridal identity is a people who have an ongoing encounter with God's affection.

Bridegroom Foundation #4—the God of Jealous Anger

The essence of God's judgment is His commitment to remove all that hinders love in our lives.

> For true and righteous are His judgments, because He has judged the great harlot who corrupted the earth with her fornication; and He has avenged on her the blood of His servants shed by her.... And I heard... the voice of a great multitude... saying, "Alleluia! For the Lord God Omnipotent reigns! Let us be glad and rejoice... for the marriage of the Lamb has come, and His wife has made herself ready."
>
> —Revelation 19:2, 6–7

This passage describes a scene in heaven related to the marriage of Jesus to His church, which takes place immediately after Jesus releases His terrifying judgments on the world system at the time of His Second Coming. As a Bridegroom God preparing His people for the great wedding day, the focus of God's jealous anger is directed in judgment of two things: first, those who gave themselves to immorality; second, those who persecuted His people. Both issues cause harm to His bride. The principle underlying His jealous anger is this: whatever harms His bride's preparation as His eternal companion will be judged.

The problem exists because immorality is practiced by some of God's own people. This creates a necessity for God's jealousy to be released toward us. God manifests His jealousy in our lives as divine discipline. Many confuse God's correction as rejection, but there is no rejection in God's discipline. Just the opposite—He disciplines us because of His passionate and jealous desire for His bride to be an equally yoked partner with Him. He will not allow anything to continue in our lives that hinders the development of our love. So because He delights in us, He disciplines us. This flows out of His passion for us, not His rejection of us.

> For whom the Lord loves He corrects, just as a father the son in whom he delights.
>
> —Proverbs 3:12

Another aspect of God's jealous anger can be seen in the way He confronts the enemies of His people. We will look closer at this aspect in a later chapter.

Bridegroom Foundation #5—the God of Fascinating Beauty

The final dimension of the Bridegroom God at which we will look is His infinite beauty. One day we will gaze upon Him for billions of years at a stretch. This description and any other will seem pitiful in its attempt to convey the reality of Him, but we must understand as well as we can that our Bridegroom possesses a beauty that transcends any other in the created realm. He is far above all other magnificence and pleasure. His endless splendor shines forth from His tenderness, gladness, and desire for us. (Indeed, it's impossible to understand His beauty without first understanding His tenderness, gladness, and desire, for His beauty radiates from them.) As we encounter it through Scripture and by His revelation in our spirits, His beauty fascinates and captivates our hearts. He woos and wows us with magnificence.

A believer struggling with deep feelings of rejection and condemnation is not free to see God's beauty in this way. A rejected spirit shuts down the ability to perceive the beauty of God that is right before your eyes. Being confident in God's love for you is necessary to seeing God's beauty.

This fascination with the God of beauty is easily the greatest source of pleasure in heaven and earth. Above all things that give the human heart pleasure, one is paramount: God revealing Himself to us personally and individually. David testified, "At Your right hand are pleasures forevermore" (Ps. 16:11). He was saying, in a way, "When I discover more of Your beauty, my spirit is completely exhilarated!" He experienced the highest pleasure known to the human heart. He lived with a fascinated heart that continually discovered new dimensions of God's magnificence. This was the single greatest attribute of his life. He drank from the well of God's endlessly unfolding beauty. King David gave insight into his heart's obsession when he testified, "One thing I ask of the LORD, this is what I seek: that I may dwell in the house of the LORD all the days of my life, to gaze upon the beauty of the LORD" (Ps. 27:4, NIV). This must also become our obsession if we are to be people after God's own heart fulfilling our destiny in this generation.

Beloved, we will have divine satisfaction forever, discovering more of His beauty through endless ages. And we can begin now! Indeed, we must begin now, for the sake of what God would have us be. He wants us to be always caught up in fascination and to become confident in love before Him; then and only then does He reveal more of His sublime beauty to us. Take one step into this realm, and you find it's impossible to exhaust His store of surprises; they unfold as you perceive more of His heart and as He reveals Himself to you in progressively greater measure. It's like a walk through an endless garden of flowers, each kind more resplendent and inventive than the one before, each path leading to waterfalls and vistas ever more breathtaking to behold. The heart of God is a wonderland, a universe of beauty like no place mankind could dream up. All beauty on earth is merely a reflection of Him; even the most beautiful thing you can think of will one day be swallowed up by the beauty of His heart like the beam of a flashlight in the intensity of a thousand suns.

Are you surprised at this new approach to holiness? It will change the very face of Christianity. It's nothing like the legalistic straitjackets of yesterday. It's rooted in strong desire, not shame; beauty, not bashing. By understanding that God desires us as His bride, our generation will arise in beauties of holiness yet unknown, with hearts ripe and sweet with passion and love. We will gladly choose Him over everything else that competes for our attention. We will count all things lost for the excellence of knowing Jesus Christ our Lord (Phil. 3:8). We will deny our flesh not primarily because of fear but out of the overflow of lovesick hearts, captured by the Man Christ Jesus, beauty incarnate. This intimacy will be motivated most of all by the astonishing revelation that He wants to marry us and have us share His gladness, pleasure, and beauty for time and beyond.

> ABOVE ALL THINGS THAT GIVE THE HUMAN HEART PLEASURE, ONE IS PARAMOUNT: GOD REVEALING HIMSELF TO US PERSONALLY AND INDIVIDUALLY.

Let's look deeper into the heart of God as David did. Let's gaze upon the divine emotions that set us on a course of passionate abandonment, becoming people with hearts after God's heart.

Chapter Three

THE GAZE THAT STUNS THE HEART

It sounds romantic to us now, but as a shepherd boy watching the flocks, David was the equivalent of a night watchman sitting in a booth and making sure nobody breaks into a storage facility. Anybody who has held a job in security knows there is nothing special about it. It's boring, unglamorous, mundane work. You sit there filing your nails, listening to the radio, counting the crickets chirping outside. You don't even want to admit to your friends that you have a job like that.

I can picture David, a young teenager sitting in the fields behind his house, playing his guitar, and biding his time. He probably smelled like sheep, his hands coated in a permanent residue of lanolin and dirt. In my imagined scene, the sheep, his only companions, huddle together and eat grass under the sun—dumb, vulnerable animals. The sun has baked the young shepherd's face, arms, and neck red. Members of a passing caravan might chuckle to see him, knowing he must be the youngest boy in the family, dealt the least favorite task of babysitting the flocks without even a roof over his head. Nobody would believe his stories about killing wild animals with his sword. Nobody cared to hear the songs he composed on his nondescript, homemade harp. His family was poor and lived in a tiny town. He was often ignored and belittled by his seven older brothers. But as he wandered those back hills of Bethlehem and looked up at the stars, something caught his attention, and he began to sing, "I don't know You very well, but I love You. I want to know You. What are You like? Who are You? What is my life about?"

What did David see? What did he find in the long hours of gazing on God's beauty in the stars and the sunsets? What did God whisper to his heart that became the foundation of who he was to become?

Behind that ruddy face, deep inside that boy's frame, was a heart unlike any the world had seen. It drew God's attention away from the cosmos, away from the majesty of the cities and oceans and natural wonders of the world. Wouldn't you love for your heart to catch God's eye as He looked upon creation? Wouldn't you love to feel His attention focused squarely on you? It happened to David. One day the Spirit of the Lord came upon the prophet Samuel and whispered in his ear, "I am replacing Saul, the rebellious king of Israel. I have found a young man who has a heart for Me. He wants the same things I want. He's a young guitar player, and I really like him. He doesn't even know I've heard his love songs in the night, but he has a heart that's hungry for the things that fill My heart. I hear his voice, and I have taken note of him. I want you to tell him what I think about him." In those sun-scorched, no-name fields behind Bethlehem, even before Samuel arrived, David was becoming a picture of the End-Time church.

Beholding and Becoming

We have looked at the threefold manner of becoming people with hearts after God's: we study the emotions of His heart, obey His commands, and contend for His fullness of power. We will develop these last two more, but let's look now at the first thing—what it means to be students of God's emotions. That leads us to one of the most important spiritual principles in life transformation. I call it the "beholding and becoming principle."

People often ask me after I teach on David's life, "How do I get a heart like David's, consumed with love for God?" I tell them that if they behold and study God's fiery love for them, their hearts will become fiery with love for God. As we behold the inner life of the Godhead, we receive divine information about what God feels about human beings, about you and me individually, about our destinies, our personalities, our likes and dislikes, our places in history. We connect with and behold the emotions of God. But more than that, we begin to change.

In 2 Corinthians 3:18, the apostle Paul referenced this spiritual principle: "But we all... beholding as in a mirror the glory of Lord, are being transformed into the same image from glory to glory." As we behold the glory of the Lord we become transformed. This very basic principle (which I highlighted in my book *Passion for Jesus*) is foundational to Paul's theology of heart transformation, and it's what made David a man after God's own heart. Simply stated, whatever we behold or understand about God's heart toward us—that's what we become in our hearts toward God. If we behold a mean and stingy God, we will become mean and stingy. But if we behold His glory, as Paul wrote, the Holy Spirit transforms us into something glorious.

As we have seen, David was a student, a Rhodes scholar, a Ph.D. of God's emotions. He was so consumed by this high endeavor that he made it his primary preoccupation "all the days of [his] life" (Ps. 27:4). In other words, he made a constant practice of beholding who God was. As a result, he had more insight into the things that burn in God's heart than any man in the Old Testament. He became different. He created his own category of intimacy with God because he dared to gaze, unafraid, at the passionate heart of God.

WHATEVER WE BEHOLD OR UNDERSTAND ABOUT GOD'S HEART TOWARD US—THAT'S WHAT WE BECOME IN OUR HEARTS TOWARD GOD.

That's what made him a man after God's heart. *That's* what brought intimacy with God—intimacy that captivated him his entire life. Beholding and becoming does the same for us. By pressing into God's heart through study and a personal pursuit of our relationship with Him, we become men and women after His heart. We experience what David experienced when he gazed upon the almost indescribable heart of God. The secret that catapulted him ahead of every other man of God in his day will be our first step toward total transformation of our lives. I'm convinced that if we beheld what David beheld about God, we would live as he lived, and we would carry our hearts before God as he did. We would become different as a result. Without even thinking about it much, we would follow in the footsteps of this ancient, yet very modern king. You see, David was no superman. The things he beheld in God's heart are still there, available to you and me as they have been available throughout history for men and women who cared to pursue Him with all their might. In fact, God invites you and me, right now, to behold the very things David did.

Beholding the Glory of God's Emotions

Paul spoke of beholding God's glory. What does this mean? As we have discovered, the greatest dimension of God's glory is His emotional life. There are many dimensions to the life of God, and nobody would presume to know or understand them all, but we know from the Bible that the very core and essence of the glory of God are the fiery emotions in the Godhead. Thus, beholding God's *emotions* is the pinnacle of beholding His *glory*. That is the process God has put in place to allow us to change into His likeness.

When we begin to understand God's emotions for us, a corresponding emotion is quickened in our hearts. The same emotions we gaze upon within His heart come alive in our own hearts, and we reciprocate them back to Him. For example, when we behold the passion in God's heart for us, our own hearts start to feel passion toward Him. In the well-known verse 1 John 4:19, John tells us that we love God because we understand that God first loved us. We could rephrase this to say we have passion for Him because we first understood His passion for us. We enjoy Jesus—why? Because we finally "get" that He enjoys us. We pursue Jesus because we grasp that He is pursuing us. We are committed and dedicated to Jesus because it hits us that He is committed and dedicated to us. The list goes on, and we could substitute many other words into this verse. The point is that our gazing into the emotions of God transforms us from the inside out.

This is a foundational biblical principle. If you want to become a fiery lover of God, then you must understand God as the fiery lover of all the ages. If you want to become passionate for God, your thoughts must be consumed with His passion for you. I regularly tell people that if they want to walk in happy holiness, they do not need to try harder but to enjoy God more. Isn't that refreshing? You don't need to dig in more, grit your teeth, and harden your resolve. The secret to having more love—or peace or joy or faith or any fruit of the Spirit—is enjoying God more. Wow! What a revelation! Trying harder will get you nowhere.

Churches are full of people who spend Monday through Saturday trying harder in their walk with the Lord. They wake up early so they can read through the Bible in a year; they make promises to themselves to invite a neighbor to church or pray for the ailing child a few doors down. They try to show the light of Christ at work and hold their tongues when angered by their spouse. Then on Sunday they cringe in the pew during worship and feel somehow that they've spent another week failing to be a good Christian. But if you experience God's enjoyment of you, then you will begin enjoying God, and this whole cycle changes. Transformation happens as naturally as the changing of seasons. You will live in much greater holiness, and you will be truly happy. You will love people and have a peaceful heart. You won't be so concerned about not doing bad things because your heart will find no pleasure in them anyway.

WE ENJOY JESUS—WHY? BECAUSE WE FINALLY "GET" THAT HE ENJOYS US.

How do we get the ball rolling on this? How do we go about enjoying God more? Remember the "behold and become principle." We enjoy God more by searching out and convincing ourselves of God's enjoyment of us. This is the path toward living in the truth of Scripture, a path that has been largely obscured and, as a result, has left the church all but desolate in places. This process of transformation never ends. What we begin now in the realm of discovering God's emotions, we will continue to do for all the ages to come. For all eternity, we will gaze on the internal workings of God's heart toward us. We will be always gazing, always discovering, always changing, always enjoying, always reflecting more of His glory and passion.

Most Christians have studied what the Bible teaches about renewing your mind, and often they come away dissatisfied, perhaps because a Sunday school teacher or pastor taught a lesson based on the "try harder" school of thought. What regular churchgoer hasn't known the feeling of leaving church and thinking, *Did anything change, or am I the same person who went in?* Beholding and becoming is the key to breaking out of that futile cycle and truly renewing your mind.

How do our hearts become alive? How do we get free from the addictions, bondages, and pain of the past? Paul taught the Colossian believers to seek renewal by receiving knowledge of the image of God (Col. 3:10). In other words, he was saying, "You experience renewal by receiving the knowledge of God's personality." Spiritual renewal and that durable transformation of the mind we all seek will only happen through the knowledge of God's heart bursting into our own hearts. That only happens when we come into contact with God and the truth about God in His Word.

Have you noticed how you can go a year or two in kind of a humdrum state, listening to the people's advice all around you, but never feeling that you have moved ahead in God? Then one day God sends one sentence from heaven to your spirit—a sentence about His opinion of you or your situation—and in an instant everything changes. He did what nobody else could do in about a fraction of a second.

What God thinks and feels about you is worth far more than the best advice from the most important people in your life. No other "wisdom" approaches it. Nothing holds greater power to transform your inner life than that moment when God's voice touches your spirit with personal revelation of who He is, who you are in light of that, and what He would have you do. It can come through the Bible as a certain passage hits you right between the eyes. It can happen in conversation, or when you're alone in the car. It might be revelation about a matter of immediacy or grave seriousness. Sometimes it's nothing more (and nothing less) than the revelation that He really enjoys being with you. That alone can change your life, if you make it a foundation of your walk with God. I believe He is always looking to give you and me an opportunity to peek inside the interior life of the Godhead, to gaze upon His burning desires, emotions, and passions. When you witness that, you are transformed—you behold and become. Such an experience can never be neutral. It awakens you to who you are, who He is, and who you will be.

WHAT GOD THINKS AND FEELS ABOUT YOU IS WORTH FAR MORE THAN THE BEST ADVICE FROM THE MOST IMPORTANT PEOPLE IN YOUR LIFE.

The Divine Partnership

There is a divine partnership in beholding and becoming men and women after God's heart. God has a role, and we have a role. God will not do our part for us. We can't do God's part for Him. Our responsibility is to *fill our minds* with the truth of God's personality—to gaze upon Him as David did. God's promise in return is to *supernaturally change our emotions*. This is the kingdom of God's division of labor. We change our minds, and God changes our hearts (meaning our emotions). Beholding God's emotions is something *only you* can do in your own secret life in God. The truths of His heart must get into the particular language of your heart. No other person can do it for you, and God Himself won't do it for you. You cannot go through a prayer line to get it. You cannot obtain it by reading a book. This is *your* division of the partnership, wholly and completely yours. It can't be hired out to any other man or woman of God.

So we must get it into our brains. We saturate our thoughts with God's emotions and His passion for us. We take the transcript of God's soul, the Word of God, and we fill our minds with it line by line, truth by truth, day after day, year after year. And we speak the Word. It comes alive much faster as it travels through our lips, especially in prayer. We begin to use the language of God's emotions in our deepest, most private dialogues with God. We begin to speak the truths of God's heart back to Him, and He transforms our emotional chemistry.

You may have discovered in this life that you don't have the power to change your emotions directly. You can't say, "Joy!" and elicit joy from your soul. You can't demand, "Gladness, rise up within me now!" It will never happen. You might get a jolt of adrenaline, but long-lasting emotions are not awakened by determination. That's *God's part* of the division of labor, and it's a supernatural work of the Spirit in us. But here's the good news: all our emotions are linked to thoughts or ideas. Correct thoughts about God bring wonderful emotions. This is why the truth sets us free (John 8:32). You can indirectly change your emotions by flooding your thoughts with the truth about God.

In the early days of my Christian life, my friends and I read Romans 12:2, about being "transformed by the renewing of your mind," in the negative sense. We thought it meant, "You will be transformed mostly by staying away from sinful movies," and we had a whole list of bad things to stay away from so that we would end up transformed. But there is much more to this principle than clamping down on ourselves and staying away from bad things. Your mind is not renewed primarily by staying away from bad things but by filling your mind with the truth about God. You don't need better sin-avoidance techniques but a new vision of what God's heart looks like. Flowing from that vision will be a new vision of what *you look like to God.* When I fill my mind with what God's emotions look like, I experience new dimensions of grace to stay away from the "bad things."

The only part that troubles me about this "beholding and becoming principle" is how few people are truly willing to give their time and energy to it. I know many believers who are serious about having their hearts and spirits renewed. Yet their main strategy is to pursue more information about God without putting it into practice. They come by the thousands to conferences, prayer lines, and Bible schools, saying, "I want passion for Jesus!" Yet it seems they will do everything except take time to behold and study God's passion for them. Though well meaning, they try to reverse the divine process of growing in love. They focus on becoming instead of beholding. They jump to step two, trying to bypass step one. They might focus on having their hearts healed or flowing with joy or peace. They glom onto every teaching that promises results, every speaker with a new approach. But you can't become until you behold. Becoming is good, but God's sequence says we must behold the reality within His heart. Then He does His part and awakens joy and peace and all the rest within us.

YOUR MIND IS NOT RENEWED PRIMARILY BY STAYING AWAY FROM BAD THINGS BUT BY FILLING YOUR MIND WITH THE TRUTH ABOUT GOD.

Transformation will not happen simply by hearing a teaching or reading a book. It has to be more than a sermon, more than a class you attend, and more than a video series you watch. You will not find the fire of love for Him by only hearing teachings that exhort you to be a fiery lover. Exhortation to action does not equip your heart to carry out that action. Have you noticed that? Exhortations to "love harder" never awaken love in your heart. A good teaching or book will arouse spiritual desire and give you the vision to go find the food for yourself. It makes you say, "I want it!" But hunger and vision are all books and sermons can offer. In and of themselves, books and sermons will never equip your heart to actually love. That change requires a lifestyle of being in the Word. If you want passion or love for God, then fill your time and your mind with the revelation of God's passion and love for you. It is uncomplicated, but few people actually live out this revelation.

Transformed Emotions and Obedience

Some years ago I began to try this very thing. I studied God's emotions. I gazed upon them in His Word. I filled my mind with them. Then I began to speak them back to the Lord in prayer. I began to use biblical language about God's heart and emotions in my private prayer life. I started to say, "God, You are filled with pleasure. You have overflowing joy, and You are exceedingly glad. You enjoy me and delight in me." I realized the Lord wants us to talk to Him about these truths even when no one is around. He invites us to open our Bibles, find out what He is like, fill our minds with specific passages that say this, and get them into our prayer dialogue. We must teach them, talk about them, sing them, and let God awaken our hearts with them.

When you read the Bible, turn it into dialogue: "Jesus, You said in Your Word here that You'll be with us to the end of the age. You said God loves us with tender compassion." When you talk in a direct way, setting your mind on Him, or beholding Him, your spirit opens up. When I began to speak these things in my own deep dialogues with God, my emotions slowly transformed.

I began to feel pleasure and joy and gladness in loving Him. When I felt His delight in me, I soon began to delight in Him and His Word as I never had before on a consistent basis.

That's the effect of gazing upon His heart. It will stabilize you in Him. You don't live like a bungee jumper, swinging up and down, side to side on a wild emotional ride. You don't live like a spelunker, hanging down in a dark cavern of negative feelings. God has given you the key to transformed emotions. Your view of God's emotions changes everything within your own emotions. Gazing upon God's soul gives you spiritual information, not neutral information. This information is powerful and full of life-changing energy. When that information hits your sincere spirit, a slow-motion explosion, orchestrated by the Holy Spirit, occurs inside you. It doesn't happen in one day but incrementally. You may take three steps forward and two steps back in the process of being renewed, yet over time, your emotions are transformed and your heart is awakened.

This is nothing less than recapturing our inheritance. Jesus promised we would have hearts that flow like a river by the supernatural work of the Holy Spirit.

> On the last day, that great day of the feast, Jesus stood and cried out, saying, "If anyone thirsts, let him come to Me and drink. He who believes in Me, as the Scripture has said, out of his heart will flow rivers of living water." But this He spoke concerning the Spirit.
>
> —John 7:37–39

The Practicality of Beholding and Becoming

When I talk about gazing upon and beholding the emotions of God, one common response I hear is that we Christians have to "be practical" and not just sit around searching out His heart. *Beholding* is viewed as peripheral or extreme—something for people who have no "real" jobs or families. Beloved, I tell you, studying the heart of God is absolutely crucial if we are to have healthy families and careers. The most practical thing you can do to take care of your family or business is to cultivate an overflowing heart. As you regularly behold the happy God in the Word, you will be progressively filled with happiness. You will take care of your family far better than if you were grouchy. Have you noticed that the blessing is much smaller for the people around you when you go about your God-ordained responsibilities with a spirit of depression, heaviness, anger, and bitterness? Grumpy, duty-bound service is better than nothing, but it is not God's best way.

But if you invest time in understanding the happiness of God's heart for you, your heart is gloriously awakened. You become powerful and effective in your duties in the kingdom of God and in all aspects of life. You serve with a happy heart, and that happiness is multiplied. Don't be one of those people who say, "I'm too busy to sit around beholding the glory of God's heart." That's like choosing to live with a locked heart. Don't buy the argument that spending time on this is not realistic or practical. In truth, there is nothing more *practical* we can do.

WHEN THAT INFORMATION HITS YOUR SINCERE SPIRIT, A SLOW-MOTION EXPLOSION, ORCHESTRATED BY THE HOLY SPIRIT, OCCURS INSIDE YOU.

To gaze upon the heart of God creates a heart flowing with His attributes. But we must come to Jesus in the way the Scriptures say, not the way our denomination or our favorite church speaker says. There are four basic requirements that I'll mention here.

A spirit of obedience

If there is even one area of rebellion against God in your life, then your heart won't flow in the way God promises. Declare war on any area of compromise in your life. You may stumble in that area, but if you are sincerely warring against it, you will still gain ground. After all, the flowing heart is what empowers you to get free from besetting sin. God doesn't require that you be free from all struggles before He releases His power in your heart. Just the opposite; the power of God helps you get free.

I am not suggesting that we are free to disobey God until our emotions change. It is the wisdom of God and the will of God that we obey Him when we don't feel like it. I believe in obedience when I don't feel like obeying. When I'm depressed and feeling horrible, I still need to obey God. However, I obey a lot more and with greater strength when my emotions are touched by the revelation of God's emotions.

There is a place and a time to exert effort and to be disciplined in the Word, yet discipline, work, and effort follow much easier after you have touched at least the beginnings of enjoyment. Lovers have always made better workers. When desire and enjoyment, even in their beginning stages, are in place, obedience seems like the only reasonable option.

Faith in God's love

You must cultivate confidence in God's affection toward you even when you stumble. If you lack this confidence, then you close your spirit toward Jesus. You cultivate condemnation and self-accusation, and that makes it impossible to grow.

The revelation that God enjoys you in your weakness transforms you. In my experience, this is the hardest revelation for people to enter into and the place on the spiritual journey where most people stall and stop. The reason? You will never enjoy God more than your revelation of God enjoying you in your weakness. Let me say it again: you will never enjoy God *more than* you experience His enjoyment of you in your weakness. But when you do see that He enjoys you in weakness, then you bear fruit. You begin to enjoy God all the time. Your heart responds in affection. You hear the Godhead, the Three in One, say, "We like you." Your heart answers, "I like You, then." Who doesn't enjoy being with people who like him? So when you understand that God likes you all the time, you respond by liking Him. You start smiling just thinking about God. It happens automatically.

WHEN DESIRE AND ENJOYMENT, EVEN IN THEIR BEGINNING STAGES, ARE IN PLACE, OBEDIENCE SEEMS LIKE THE ONLY REASONABLE OPTION.

Then another miraculous thing happens: you begin to enjoy yourself. You begin to like you. You prefer to be yourself over any other person on Earth. This is a revolutionary change for most people. A woman prayed earnestly, "Lord, I want to love my neighbor like I love myself." The Lord surprised her with His answer: "That's the problem—you do. You despise yourself; therefore, you despise your neighbor."

It is God's will that you would come to the transforming summit of self-acceptance on your journey. He wants you to inhabit this place of personal enjoyment and satisfaction. It's a position where, in the secrecy of your own heart, you would rather be who you are than anybody else. That gives you incredible confidence and desire to enjoy and love others. Fireworks go off inside you; streams of life touch your being. There's nothing like waking up in your own skin and thinking, *I'm glad I am who I am. Thank You, Lord!*

A spirit of servanthood

The prophet Isaiah said that if we extend our souls for others, then our hearts would be like a well-watered garden (Isa. 58:10–11). Some of God's people carefully guard their lives from all inconvenience and only contribute as long as their comfort zone isn't disturbed. But we must give ourselves away to God's people as servants of God's purpose. Jesus said the greatest among us would be the servant of all. We can't gaze into the heart of God and retain a "me first" attitude.

A spirit of devotion

This means Bible study and Christian service, cultivating a dialogue with Jesus as we devote ourselves to His Word and the practice of His Word. We release the "I love You, Jesus" in our spirit toward God as we study the Scriptures or serve in the home, marketplace, or church. We become devoted to the things and people He is devoted to.

IT IS GOD'S WILL THAT YOU WOULD COME TO THE TRANSFORMING SUMMIT OF SELF-ACCEPTANCE ON YOUR JOURNEY.

Information and revelation about the inner life of the Godhead should be a major pursuit in our training and ministry. It should be the focus of our relationships and all types of outreaches. We need knowledge of God's heart much more than we have today. So do the people around us who have no idea Jesus loves them. We must know what He is feeling and be able to express that to others if we are to be the people He wants, doing the exploits He has in mind for us to do. We must gaze on His heart and let it transform us.

Our view of God's emotional life sets the course for how we relate to Him, what we think of ourselves, what we think of others—the whole basis for how we live and serve Christ. The secrets of our Father's character are in the Word of God, and they are revealed to us through communion with Him by the Holy Spirit, who brings them alive in our hearts. There is much more to this study of the glad heart of God that will free us from the bondage of false beliefs. We'll see that in the next chapter.

4

Chapter Four

IS GOD MOSTLY MAD, GLAD, OR SAD?

Here's a question: How does God feel most of the time? Is He bored? Worried? Blasé? Happy? Concerned? Detached? Engaged? Mad, glad, or sad? It sounds lighthearted, but it's one of the most important questions of our entire spiritual journey. How does God feel when He looks at you? What wells up in His heart when His eyes turn upon your life? I have asked many people this question over the years, and they usually respond in one of two ways:

- God is mostly mad.
- God is mostly sad.

And in both cases, they think it's their fault. Many Christians believe very strongly that God is angry and grieved with each of us. In some parts of the body of Christ, this sentiment is expressed clearly and openly, but in most quarters it's inarticulate. It's one of those under-the-surface, sinister opinions everybody holds, but nobody talks about. God is viewed as distant, angry, sitting on the throne, and spending the bulk of His emotional energy being disappointed in mankind. We picture a weeping God who beats His breast and turns His eyes away from us in shame. But Scripture tells us the very opposite. Our God smiles and rejoices. His emotions fall into a third category:

- God is mostly glad.

That is the only correct answer! Moses, under the prophetic anointing, made a stunning declaration about the Lord's gladness: "The LORD your God will make you abound in all the work of your hand.... For the LORD will again rejoice over you for good as He rejoiced over your fathers" (Deut. 30:9). In this passage, God was telling Moses that at the end of the age God will break forth with rejoicing over His people. He will reveal Himself to them as the glad God who overflows with delight and enjoyment. Instead of cowering at the feet of an angry God, the body of Christ will bask in the sunshine of His gladness.

THIS ISN'T JUST DRY EXHORTATION TO BE GLAD, BUT THE EXPERIENTIAL UNDERSTANDING OF HIS GLADNESS FOR US. THAT GLADNESS IS CATCHING!

This is the day we are living in!

If this picture of God seems impossible to you, scan the Word. Passages about God's gladness abound throughout the Bible. For example, Zephaniah 3:17 reveals Him as One who rejoices: "He will take great delight in you, he will quiet you with his love, he will rejoice over you with singing" (NIV). Imagine that! He will sing and rejoice over His people with gladness. He will quiet our stormy hearts with the revelation of His love. God's songs over His people are not songs of anger but of rejoicing and tender love. In this passage, He is not just exhorting people to be glad, but He is promising to sing songs that make us glad. These songs reveal His affectionate heart for us. This isn't just dry exhortation to be glad, but the experiential understanding of His gladness for us. That gladness is catching!

The rest of the Book of Zephaniah lays the backdrop for this divine promise. It describes the scenes at the end of the age when everything that can be shaken is being shaken. In that day, men will literally die of heart attacks because of fear (Luke 21:26). Fear will be one of the predominant emotions worldwide. In the midst of this dramatic shaking, God promises that He will comfort and quiet His people by releasing songs of His *affection* and *gladness*. We will be calmed on the inside by this revelation. Intimacy with a glad God will nourish our souls and sustain the church in the midst of unprecedented calamity. Like a parent with a troubled child, God will sing love songs that soothe us and impart His delight to us.

I have already said I believe the greatest dimension of God's glory is His emotions, and now we begin to see that central to His emotional life are His gladness and joy. This is what God communicated to Moses when he longed to see God's glory. God promised to make known His glory and goodness to him by revealing His compassion (Exod. 33:18–19). Next, God declared His glory as being "the LORD, the LORD God, merciful and gracious, longsuffering, and abounding in goodness and truth, keeping mercy for thousands" (Exod. 34:6–7). Notice that when God reveals His glory, He emphasizes the glory of His emotions. As we enter into the reality of His happiness and joy, our hearts discover other emotions that abound in His heart. We begin to experience His desires for us, His beauty, and His pleasures. But we cannot skip the foundational step of understanding His gladness. We will not easily believe that God burns with desire for us or that He is exceedingly beautiful if we do not first believe that He is *glad*. It must be the foundation of our theology: our *God* is a God who smiles.

God's heart is infinitely glad in the fellowship of the Trinity. Jesus perpetually rejoices before the Father. He describes Himself at Creation, saying, "Then I was beside Him as a master craftsman; and I was daily His delight, rejoicing always before Him" (Prov. 8:30). In this passage, Jesus, who is the personification of wisdom, was at the right hand of God the Father. In His wisdom, He possessed overflowing delight and gladness while He created. Scripture says God creates not out of duty or boredom but out of His pleasure (Rev. 4:11). A great ocean of delight resides within His personality. This is the God that holds us in His gaze and the God we gaze upon and behold. And He is, above all, glad.

HE CELEBRATES YOU OR ME AS HIS CHILD AND THROWS A PARTY IN OUR HONOR.

If at the center of your theology is a God who smiles, then it is not hard to understand this next truth about Him: *He is smiling at you as you respond to Him in willing obedience.* His infinite smile extends over His creation. He is delighted in Himself and in the overflow of that delight, but He especially enjoys humans who respond to the grace He offered freely in Christ Jesus. This applies to each of us individually and uniquely. God has affection and enjoyment for you even at your weakest point.

> For the LORD takes pleasure in His people; He will beautify the humble with salvation.
>
> —PSALM 149:4

He actually enjoys you! What a powerful concept! Not only does He smile, but also He smiles when He looks at you! Most people struggle to imagine this because they never quite grasp the first premise: that He is a smiling God. They only perceive a God who frowns with disappointment most of the time. When they hear that He is smiling and rejoicing over them, it's like the words mean nothing to them. The truth goes right over their heads. They can't reconcile this with their picture of a dour Deity who turns His eyes on them and scowls.

In Proverbs 8:31 Jesus describes Himself as One rejoicing in the inhabited world and experiencing delight in the sons of men. Though His delight in us is so clearly stated in Scripture, we find ourselves like the prodigal son who was confused by his father's overwhelming delight: we stand at a distance, not knowing how to receive it. It's more logical and comfortable for us to bring our list of failures and then plead for a low position in His kingdom. Yet instead of negotiating with us, He embraces us with unabashed affection and covers us with the royal robe of righteousness. He celebrates you or me as His child and throws a party in our honor. This is the God we serve. This is who He is regardless of what we do.

Throne of Gladness and Pleasure

Around the throne of God is an atmosphere saturated with gladness and rejoicing. The closer you get to the Person of God, the more gladness you experience. King David, the great theologian of the pleasure of God, described this joyful environment around God's throne in one of his songs: "Honor and majesty are before Him; strength and gladness are in His place" (1 Chron. 16:27). He testified first of God's majesty and power and then of the gladness that surrounds the throne. In His presence is fullness of joy. Happiness prevails everywhere in heaven. Jesus referred to this joy as being His at creation (Prov. 8:30). David had this incredible revelation that the atmosphere around the throne of God was full of gladness. His heart overflowed when he cried, "In Your presence is fullness of joy; at Your right hand are pleasures forevermore" (Ps. 16:11). He was exclaiming, "Let me tell you about the God I love. He overflows with gladness!"

The One seated on the throne is glad, and all those that stand near Him are swept up in joyful contagion of His gladness. The closer we get to His throne in heaven, the happier we become. Job said that when God was creating the world, the angels, referred to as "the sons of God," were filled with happiness as they sang. They were over-the-top exhilarated (Job 38:7). God even created angels with a capacity for happiness—a phenomenal reality!

In my imagination I can see the Father looking at the Son with a big grin as they planned Creation. I see Jesus smiling and asking, "Well, Father, what kind of servants should We create for My bride?" The Father replies, "Happy servants." So God placed the capacity for happiness in their very design. In Luke 2, these very angels appeared in the heavens to tell people that God had supplied a remedy—a Savior—to bring us back into fellowship with Him. The choirs of heaven and the angels appeared and were almost unable to contain their glee. They sang it loud and long, "Hosanna! Glory to God in the highest!" They trumpeted the good news that God was removing the barriers so people could come into one-heart fellowship with Him. This wasn't a one-time celebration but a lifestyle of heaven being revealed for a moment to citizens of Earth. Jesus tells us there is joy in the presence of the angels when one sinner repents (Luke 15:10). They shout, "This is wonderful! Another one! Let's celebrate." And this type of joy goes on and on, and it will continue forever.

SMILING IN HEAVEN IS NOT REQUIRED—IT'S INEVITABLE.

What kind of God would put happiness at the very core of the servants of the house? Only a God who is happy Himself. If God were always angry, surely His servants would always be angry. If God were vengeful, surely His servants would be a vengeful army, not a singing choir that suddenly appears in the heavens. Angels have happy hearts because God has a happy heart.

And the angels aren't the only ones. In my mind's eye I can see the elders who sit before Him falling down to worship as they are caught up in awe with gladness before God's throne (Rev. 11:16). I imagine that one day I'll get to approach one of them and inquire, "Excuse me, I know you are worshiping, but I want to know one thing: how are you feeling?" I imagine he will rise and respond, "The closer we get to the throne, the more joy we feel! The more we see of Him, the more delight we experience! It's fantastic! I can't get enough."

In God's presence, around His throne is the fullness of joy, and one day we will witness it for ourselves! The angels in His presence are full of joy. The elders are overcome with bliss. Jesus, at the right hand of the Father, brims and overflows with happiness. The Father loves His kingdom, His angels, and His people! He is a happy God!

And—wonder of wonders—God calls us to partake of this joy. In Psalm 36:8, David says to God the Father, "You give them drink from the river of Your pleasures." By giving us drink, David means God shares the pleasure of His Being with us. There is simply no greater pleasure than when *God* reveals *God* to the human spirit. It happens now on Earth to a certain degree for those of us who are His children, and it will happen in heaven in exponentially greater measure. When we see Him face-to-face we will voluntarily rejoice.

It's not as if we will enter heaven and receive an injection of laughing gas. That's not how it works. Smiling in heaven is not required—it's inevitable. There are no happy robots. Happiness is the province of people who choose of their own free will to enter into it. We will see something (and Someone) that makes us extraordinarily glad. We will marvel at the streets of gold, the incredible opulence of our surroundings in that heavenly city. We will feel things that far surpass what we have felt before. If you and I could be instantly transported to the throne of God, we would be shocked by the happiness that would overcome us. We would experience a combination of overwhelming terror of God's majesty and an overflowing happiness. We would cry, "More! But I can't take more! Too much! Never enough! It's so intense, I can't stand it! Oh, but I want more!"

Responding to the God of Gladness

This doctrine of God's gladness isn't a theological curiosity meant to entertain us. It is foundational to helping our hearts grow into spiritual maturity. Deuteronomy 28:47–48 says:

> Because you did not serve the LORD your God with joy and gladness of heart, for the abundance of everything, therefore you shall serve your enemies.

When we enter into God's joy and gladness, the door to much of Satan's activity slams shut in our lives. The joy of serving God keeps us from compromise. A glad heart is a strong heart. The Bible says the joy of the Lord is our strength (Neh. 8:10). And don't get the wrong idea about the above verse from Deuteronomy. God is not acting out of spite. He's not pouting and saying, "I was glad, and you would not enter into My gladness, so forget it. You're going to serve your enemies. Now you're really going to hurt." Rather, He is laying out the only two options that exist. Either we enter into His gladness with whole hearts, or we will eventually come under the influence of the enemy, giving in to his accusations, becoming offended at God.

As the dominos fall after we are offended, we end up serving the lies of the enemy instead of living beneath the truths of God. We see God as different than He is. We imbibe false notions about Him. We give ear to the whispers of the devil that malign His character. If we continue to agree with the enemy, he easily leads us into compromise and darkness. It happens to believers and nonbelievers alike.

The antidote is to live in the reality of God's joy and gladness. That's how the End-Time church will be empowered, set apart, and strong. Psalm 2:11 illustrates this principle with a wonderful picture. In the time of the End-Time judgments, God says, "Kiss the Son, lest He be angry, and you perish in the way." If we don't kiss the Son, meaning enter into intimacy with Him, we will eventually fall prey to an accusing spirit against God because of His judgments. Don't you see the enemy's tactic? He tries to align us with himself and bring us into opposition to the Lord by unleashing accusations against Him. If we accept the enemy's logic, it brings God's wrath upon us. Intimacy with God is the only divine plan we have for avoiding this. God does not give us the option to live in the gray zone. We will be people who are lovesick and glad before our God, or we will become angry with Him, especially in light of the intensity of His End-Time judgments. There will not be a middle ground.

Unfortunately, accusation against the character of God is lodged in the hearts of people within the body of Christ all over the earth. We believe a network of lies about God's personality. We have drunk Satan's accusations and slander against God and drawn a false picture of God. We approach the Father feeling that He is deeply grieved or angry with us because of our immaturity. We believe this because, contrary to Scripture, we think He possesses no gladness in His being. This false view of God will lead us directly into the enemy's camp. But God has gone out of His way to rescue us. The blood of Christ is our free pass into the gladness of God. Jesus died not out of anger or exasperation, but to make a way for us to enter into the Father's gladness. The Lord wants to dislodge every false accusation in our hearts against the truth of His personality. He would have us experience His happy heart so our hearts might be realigned, transformed, strengthened, matured, and renewed.

The Glad-Hearted Judge

Take this little self-test: what emotions would you feel if your final evaluation were tonight? Imagine that an angel is scheduled to arrive in thirty minutes to tell you the exact judgment of God over your life. What feelings surge to the fore of your heart? Most people would admit a feeling of dread. They think to themselves, *I'm in serious trouble.* But even when God judges us, He doesn't fume with frustration and anger.

In 1 Corinthians 4:5, Paul described this aspect of God: the glad-hearted Judge. Paul was addressing the Corinthians, the most carnal church we know of in the first century. Only the Laodiceans in the next generation rivaled them in carnality. Paul exhorted the Corinthians, "Do not judge anything before the time when the Lord comes." In other words, "Don't make final evaluations toward people or even yourselves." He distrusted his inability to accurately judge even his own heart. Then he dropped a bomb by telling the Corinthians that God will someday reveal the things hidden in darkness and in the secret counsels of their hearts. You can almost hear the gasp: "Oh no! We're in for some big-time punishment." Yet they had not heard Paul's full message. In the next sentence he zigged when they thought he was going to zag: "Then each one's praise will come from God." Each one's praise?

When we think about God revealing the dark things and the hidden counsels of our hearts, we think *rebuke* and immediately recoil. "Oh no, not the hidden counsels!" we say, assuming that hidden things are dark and ungodly. But God says the opposite. Hidden within our hearts are not just shameful things but many good things, like the deep cry to be totally God's. Deep inside we fight to be fully His against all opposition of the enemy. Only God fully perceives the depth of this longing of our heart. And the good news is that on the last day He will reveal it and give us praise for it. The *yes* in our spirit is an imperfect *yes*, but it is a *yes*. It is the very work of God Himself in us. It is His supernatural activity in our inner man. He perceives our willing spirit in the struggle. He is pleased with the longings of sincere believers to be fully His. In other words, this is the essence of the real you. While we may define themselves by our failures, God defines us through His grace and by the sincere movements of our hearts, which we may not even fully understand.

HE WOULD HAVE US EXPERIENCE HIS HAPPY HEART SO OUR HEARTS MIGHT BE REALIGNED, TRANSFORMED, STRENGTHENED, MATURED, AND RENEWED.

God's Gladness in Our Deliverance

I touched earlier on a truth that bears repeating here: God smiles upon us and enjoys us though we are yet spiritually immature. Too many of us judge ourselves prematurely. Most believers only expect to love themselves when they get to heaven, when they are fully free from struggles and fully mature in love. They imagine the resurrection as the day they will finally be free, the day God will be fully happy with them, the day they will achieve full acceptance by the Godhead. They long for that day because they haven't allowed themselves to experience God's enjoyment in them now. Beloved, we don't have to wait! We have His enjoyment at this very moment. Sincere love always starts out weak. You don't become a believer on Tuesday, and by Wednesday your love for Jesus is fully established. Love is sincere and genuine many years before it becomes mature and strong.

In Luke 15, Jesus addressed angry Pharisees who were miffed at Him for eating with and fellowshiping with sinners. In reply, Jesus said His Father rejoiced and the angels that did His bidding were glad; therefore, we ought to be glad. Over and over in this chapter Jesus revealed the joyous atmosphere around the throne. In verse 10, He said, "I say to you, there is joy in the presence of the angels of God over one sinner who repents." He was speaking of the repenting sinner who is still very immature. If the sinner repents at 3:00 in the afternoon, the angels are singing and rejoicing by 3:01. That sinner is still profoundly immature in his faith, but the angels are abundantly glad. His repentance is absolutely sincere though his maturity is nonexistent. The *yes* in his spirit is imperfect, but it is eternally significant.

WHILE WE MAY DEFINE THEMSELVES BY OUR FAILURES, GOD DEFINES US THROUGH HIS GRACE.

God does not say to the sinner, "You have sincerely repented, but look at all these unsettled issues in your life. We will see how you do. Come on in, I guess, but we will be keeping a close eye on you." We think God is this way because we ourselves are this way. People clap with excitement the day a man gets saved and testifies of his desire to leave his old ways and follow the Lord. They cheer and shout, "Praise the Lord! It's real! It counts!" But within a few months, the same crowd is ready to censure him for issues of immaturity they see in his life. Within days their theology changes, and they no longer delight over his growing faith.

They turn into grumpy Pharisees, saying, "Bah humbug! Get it right. We're keeping our eye on you now."

The Lord says the opposite: "I delight in you when you have zero maturity." Remember, God can enjoy you even while disapproving of an area of sin in your life. He surely disapproves of any number of things you and I do, but that doesn't interrupt His enjoyment. If His gladness were based on our performance, He would be a sad God indeed! But the Scripture proclaims that "whom the LORD loves He corrects, just as a father the son in whom he delights" (Prov. 3:12).

Our own patience is so insufficient. We spot one thing we disapprove of in another believer's life, and then we struggle to enjoy him. He may have a good history with us, but we push him away because of one or two things that bother us. That is the limit of our patience. We feel justified in kicking people out of our hearts and lives when they bother us. Why? Because we secretly believe that God does that to us. This is not the heart of God. When the Lord finds something about our character that bothers Him, He doesn't cut us out of His heart. Rather, He is filled with patience and slow to anger. He does not reject us when something awful in our character comes to light.

When Jesus told the story of the prodigal son in Luke 15, He revealed to the religious leaders what God's emotions are like. The leaders of Jesus' day were very much like the leaders of the body of Christ today. They had totally wrong ideas about the way God feels.

> Jesus continued: "There was a man who had two sons. The younger one said to his father, 'Father, give me my share of the estate.' So he divided his property between them.
>
> "Not long after that, the younger son got together all he had, set off for a distant country and there squandered his wealth in wild living. After he

had spent everything, there was a severe famine in that whole country, and he began to be in need. So he went and hired himself out to a citizen of that country, who sent him to his fields to feed pigs. He longed to fill his stomach with the pods that the pigs were eating, but no one gave him anything.

"When he came to his senses, he said, 'How many of my father's hired men have food to spare, and here I am starving to death! I will set out and go back to my father and say to him: Father, I have sinned against heaven and against you. I am no longer worthy to be called your son; make me like one of your hired men.' So he got up and went to his father.

"But while he was still a long way off, his father saw him and was filled with compassion for him; he ran to his son, threw his arms around him and kissed him.

"The son said to him, 'Father, I have sinned against heaven and against you. I am no longer worthy to be called your son.'

"But the father said to his servants, 'Quick! Bring the best robe and put it on him. Put a ring on his finger and sandals on his feet. Bring the fattened calf and kill it. Let's have a feast and celebrate. For this son of mine was dead and is alive again; he was lost and is found.' So they began to celebrate.

"Meanwhile, the older son was in the field. When he came near the house, he heard music and dancing. So he called one of the servants and asked him what was going on. 'Your brother has come,' he replied, 'and your father has killed the fattened calf because he has him back safe and sound.'

"The older brother became angry and refused to go in. So his father went out and pleaded with him. But he answered his father, 'Look! All these years I've been slaving for you and never disobeyed your orders. Yet you never gave me even a young goat so I could celebrate with my friends. But when this son of yours who has squandered your property with prostitutes comes home, you kill the fattened calf for him!'

"'My son,' the father said, 'you are always with me, and everything I have is yours. But we had to celebrate and be glad, because this brother of yours was dead and is alive again; he was lost and is found.'"

—LUKE 15:11–32, NIV

When He told this parable, the Pharisees were extremely nervous. They knew Jesus was talking about the personality of His heavenly Father, but that picture did not work within their religious system. Their whole careers were based on a God who was mostly mad and mostly sad, but *never* glad.

The father told his servants, "Let us be glad." This is God's command to all His servants about this returning son. We can't imagine being glad when the son's motives are so obviously off. We lean toward putting him on probation and watching him carefully for a year, and then throwing a party after all goes well. In the meantime, it seems best to us to take notes on his behavior and scrutinize him to discern if he is sincere. But the Father takes the opposite approach. He celebrates immediately.

> THE PRODIGAL WAS A BELIEVER LIVING FOOLISHLY BEFORE GOD, AND JESUS WAS TEACHING HIS CHURCH HOW TO RESPOND TO THOSE BROTHERS OR SISTERS WHO STUMBLE.

In verse 28, the older, religious brother refused to join the celebration, so his father approached him and pleaded with him to join the party. This elder brother would have made a good leader in most churches today. He kept all the rules. He tried very hard, yet he never knew what it meant to *enjoy* his father at the heart level. He was angry and would not go to the party. The father begged his religious son to understand his heart.

Again, the Lord speaks to us in this verse, saying, "Please, My leaders, understand My gladness for the recovery of broken people." The leaders of the church say, "They are selfish. They just want free forgiveness." The Father says, "I know. I will conquer them with My love! I will transform them by My kindness!" In this parable, the Father is pleading with His church to celebrate the homecoming of broken people. In verse 32, the father looks at his religious son and says one of the most powerful statements in the kingdom of God: "It was right that we should make merry and be glad, for your brother was dead and is alive again, and was lost and is found."

This is often called the parable of the prodigal son, but it's primarily about a father who lost his son and what he did when his son returned. It's describing the proper dynamics of a functioning family. We apply this to unbelievers, but the primary point is God's strategy in recovering His own lost children. Jesus was talking about a son, someone inside the family of God, who wasted an anointing and an inheritance. The prodigal was a believer living foolishly before God, and Jesus was teaching His church how to respond to those brothers or sisters who stumble. We all know what to do when a new convert comes into the kingdom. We rejoice and throw a party. Yet we don't easily enter into God's gladness when one of our brothers stumbles or, far worse, when we ourselves stumble. And yet our ability to enter into God's patience and lovingkindness when we stumble is determined by how much patience and lovingkindness we have toward a brother or sister who stumbles.

What About Holiness?

Some would ask if I have gone too far, portraying God as too lenient. When believers blow it, are we right to "reward" them as the father did the prodigal son? What about holiness? I am deeply committed to holiness, and yet I believe there is only one kind: *happy holiness*. Religious, cranky holiness doesn't work. "I'm-in-a-bad-mood" holiness has no sustaining power. Happy holiness has all the power in the world. Though we experience times of true repenting and weeping over sin when we stumble and fail, our Father runs to us with a heart to restore us.

This was the case when Jesus, blazing holiness Himself, walked the earth. He drew sinners to Himself and fellowshiped with them. He was the exact representation of the heart of the Father (Heb. 1:3). He walked in perfected holiness that could not be improved upon, and He still enjoyed the company of people with imperfect holiness. That means that the more we are separated to Him in holiness, the more our hearts will enjoy the weakest believer's journey into mature love. It sounds like a contradiction, but it's the example Jesus set. In Psalm 60:6, David said, "God has spoken in His holiness: 'I will rejoice.'" The gladness and holiness in God's heart are not opposed to each other; David said they are one and the same thing. God's gladness is an expression of His holiness, and vice versa. This is called *holy gladness,* and it leads to happy holiness.

> CRANKY HOLINESS IS USUALLY THE RESULT OF LIVING WITH A WOUNDED AND REJECTED SPIRIT WHILE SEEKING TO LIVE RIGHT IN YOUR OWN STRENGTH.

Happy holiness speaks of a transformed heart of obedience that is the overflow of encountering the gladness of God's heart.

We become glad with His gladness, and this energizes our life of holiness. Some of the traditional approaches to holiness lead to what I call "cranky holiness," which is an outward form of holiness without an invigorated heart. Cranky holiness is usually the result of living with a wounded and rejected spirit while seeking to live right in your own strength.

It's time to throw away our religious negotiations to earn our way back into His embrace. We must shatter false paradigms of what He is like. We will never earn His favor through our religious lists or our attainment of maturity. We have His enjoyment right now, and it is that very enjoyment that will carry us through our stumbling.

It is difficult for us to imagine what the Father's gladness looks like in people. That's why He gave us a perfect representation of His gladness as a Man. Let's look now at Jesus, the happiest Man ever to walk the earth (Ps. 45:7).

Chapter Five

THE GLAD HEART OF GOD

I often wonder what Jesus was thinking the days before His crucifixion. How did He stay focused? What was on His mind? What mattered to Him in those moments?

The Bible answers this for us in part. When Jesus came into Jerusalem for the last time, He carried a message in His heart. I believe He had waited three and one-half years to share this message. It was one of the deepest things on His heart. The essence of His last public sermon was, "There is a King—My Father—who is preparing a wedding for His Son." (See Matthew 22:2.) With this, Jesus looked toward one of the greatest events of all history: the wedding supper of the Lamb (Rev. 19:1–9). His heart was caught up in that glorious future day, the great bridal feast. Emotion must have surged in His heart as He opened the treasury of this parable to the crowds. He was revealing one of the primary reasons for the cross, which would secure the inheritance His Father had promised Him—an equally yoked companion, a bride.

What Jesus accomplished on the cross is exceedingly powerful. But why He did what He did is just as stunning. What motivation beat in His heart as He endured the cross? What burned in His emotions? What was the divine logic behind the event? Simply put, He longed to be united with His bride. He burned with desire for human beings. Any bridegroom who plans a wedding knows the feeling. The Bible even gives us a glimpse into the gladness of Jesus' heart on His wedding day in the Song of Solomon.

> Go forth, O daughters of Zion, and see [the King]... on the day of his wedding, the day of the gladness of his heart.
>
> —Song of Solomon 3:11

This natural love song depicting the beauty of married love is an excellent picture of the spiritual love between Jesus and His church. The cross was motivated by a God who had great gladness about His wedding day. The plan of redemption flows from a God who eagerly anticipates the intimacy He will have with His people for eternity. The cross became a reality because, from before the beginning of time, He desired to marry us.

The Exceeding Gladness of Jesus

Our Bridegroom is, like the Father, exceedingly glad. Peter describes Jesus enduring the cross, and then he supplies the answer for what sustained Him.

> For David says concerning Him [Jesus]: "I foresaw the Lord always before My face, for He is at My right hand, that I may not be shaken. Therefore My heart rejoiced, and My tongue was glad.... You [Father] have made

known to Me [Jesus] the ways of life; You will make Me full of joy in Your presence."

—ACTS 2:25–28

In this passage, Peter described three attributes of Jesus' heart by quoting David's words from Psalm 16:8–11:

- Jesus had a rejoicing heart.
- Jesus had a glad tongue.
- Jesus is full of pleasure.

Peter took this psalm of David and interpreted it as a dialogue between Jesus and the Father. Jesus told us that He would not be shaken by the torment of the cross because the Father was at His right hand. His heart rejoiced, and His tongue was glad. The Father made Him full of joy in His presence. David was speaking of himself when he penned this psalm, yet on the Day of Pentecost Peter, under the anointing of the Spirit, reinterpreted this passage as being mostly about Christ Jesus. It was given to David so we could see into the heart of the King of kings and what He experienced in the cross and resurrection.

THE PLAN OF REDEMPTIONS FLOWS FROM A GOD WHO EAGERLY ANTICIPATES THE INTIMACY HE WILL HAVE WITH HIS PEOPLE FOR ETERNITY.

These two passages combined, Psalm 16:8–11 and Acts 2:25–28, give apostolic insight into the personality of the Godhead. We gain deep insight into Jesus' internal makeup. Jesus is the exact representation of His Father's glory and personality (Heb. 1:3). Therefore, we know what the Father's heart is like when we see Jesus' heart. Let's look into Jesus' personality in light of these two passages.

The Rejoicing Heart of Jesus

The first truth we find about Jesus in this passage is that He has a rejoicing heart rooted in the eternal reality of who He is. When Jesus said, "My heart is glad, and My glory rejoices" in Psalm 16:9, it was not a momentary happiness at His resurrection. His gladness didn't even begin with His humanity. Though His gladness was *expressed* in His humanity and conveyed in His resurrection, it sprung from an infinite well of gladness that ran through eternity. Jesus is the same yesterday, today, and forever, and therefore He rejoices and has always rejoiced.

HE LOVES TO SHOCK HIS BABES WITH HOW GOOD HE WILL BE TO THEM!

Psalm 45:7 tells us that Jesus was anointed with gladness more than any other man. The writer of Hebrews quoted Psalm 45 and assured us it speaks of the Man Christ Jesus.

> But to the Son He says: "Your throne, O God, is forever and ever.... You have loved righteousness and hated lawlessness; therefore God, Your God, has anointed You with the oil of gladness more than Your companions."
>
> —HEBREWS 1:8–9

We discover that Jesus possesses more gladness than any of His companions or fellow human beings from all of history. He was anointed with the oil of His Father's own gladness, and He had more of it than any other person who ever existed. Yes, He knew anger, grief, and sorrow. But His gladness resonated more fully than any of these. It was His dominant emotion. The Father could point to Jesus and say, "Look at My Son—His heart is just like Mine! The way He feels is how *I* feel!"

Imagine, if you can, what it was like when Jesus entered a village of Israel during His earthly ministry. I see the kids making a beeline to Him, invited by His smile and His eyes alive with pleasure. They adored the carpenter from Nazareth, the new preacher in town. You can't fool kids. If you are mean, they avoid you, even if you try to act nice. Notice they seemed to have passed up the disciples. Peter, James, and John stood around wearing their new "Disciple of Jesus" badges, thinking they were hot stuff, but the kids gave them wide berth. The same went for the mean-looking Pharisees. The idea of hugging them was absurd and, frankly, frightening.

Jesus wanted those kids around Him. They bypassed the sacred boundary lines and ran straight into His embrace. They didn't care that He was in the middle of a healing crusade. I can imagine their arms around His neck, their moms chasing after them with blood pressure rising: "Stop doing that! He's a famous preacher; you can't just grab Him!" I imagine later they talked of it over the dinner table. "Why did you go running like that to Jesus? You didn't even ask His permission."

"Mom, I can tell He likes me," the kids would reply. "He winked at me earlier. Plus, He's just nice!"

"Yeah," another would say, "and when He came into town and all the big shots were there, He looked over at me, and it seemed like He wanted to leave them behind and be with me most of all."

Luke wrote, "In that hour Jesus rejoiced in the Spirit and said, "I thank You, Father... that You have hidden these things from the wise and prudent and revealed them to babes" (Luke 10:21).

What I would give to see the Son of God overflowing with happiness and delight like that! How great is His joy when immature people receive revelation. He loves to shock His babes with how good He will be to them!

The Glad Tongue of Jesus

The second insight about the heart of Jesus found in the parallel passages of Psalm 16:8–11 and Acts 2:25–28 is that the words of His mouth are glad. He has a glad tongue. We are in error if we believe that the words of Jesus' mouth are mostly severe. Yes, He can speak with great severity, but when He speaks to His own, it's mostly with tenderness. In Psalm 16:9, this same reality is phrased, "My glory rejoices." Isn't it fantastic that the Judge of all the living and the dead is a happy Person? Wouldn't it be terrible if He spoke with sharp bitterness, anger, and out of a foul mood? But He doesn't. His speech is round and fat with gladness and happiness. His tongue is sweet and loving. Again, this truth about Jesus reflects His Father perfectly. Jesus had a glad tongue, so the Father has a glad tongue. They both carry a glow in Their voices when they speak, and beloved, so will we.

In Revelation 19:6–7 we see the great company of billions of believers gathered together on the sea of glass for the long-awaited wedding day. It's significant that human history ends with the marriage supper of the Lamb, one of the very few corporate responses of the church to Jesus described in the Word of God. On that last day we will have fully understood Jesus' leadership over history. His perfect leadership will have produced a bride that says with a *glad tongue,* "Rejoice and be glad, for the marriage of the Lamb has come!" In other words, the bride is exceedingly happy when all the information is laid out and we see that God arranged human circumstances, seasons, and events. We will rejoice with absolute gladness. We will erupt with joy.

Under the leadership of Jesus, the human heart always erupts with joy. Isaiah said that when we understand more fully, we will become radiant and our hearts shall swell with joy (Isa. 60:5). This is His desire for us even on this side of eternity. When Jesus has His way, He makes hearts glad. The apostle Jude says, "Now to

Him who is able to keep you from stumbling, and to present you faultless before the presence of His glory with exceeding joy" (Jude 24).

Can you believe this? Jesus has the ability and intention to present you with exceeding joy before the Father. On that final day I can imagine an angel greeting me and saying, "So, what do you think? It's Judgment Day. Any nerves?"

I'll answer, "Nerves? Nah, I love being here!"

He might answer, "This is the last day when all will be revealed. You will soon be presented before God. Everything you have done will be laid in the open."

I'll say, "I know it! I deeply regret some things about the way I lived my earthly life, but I'm about to see Him face-to-face. He is beautiful and full of great gladness. I have waited for this moment all of my life." We should anticipate heaven as a place of supreme gladness.

How about you? Do you cringe when you think of that day? Are you worried about what everyone will learn about your life? Do you fear that God will rebuke you publicly, before all the saints? What is your dominant emotion when you envision that day? If it is fear or dread, what does that say about your image of God? Have you fallen for lies of the devil and accepted a false view of a vindictive, unsmiling Savior? Do you wish you could find some broom closet and wait out the Judgment, coming out when the day of reckoning has passed?

> GOD IS THE AUTHOR OF REAL PLEASURE. IT SPRINGS FROM HIS VERY PERSONALITY.

Or do you picture yourself running and embracing the Lord? Does your heart skip a beat with anticipation? Do you picture His goodness outweighing and outlasting His anger? Do you see the Judgment as revealing the good motives of your heart, too?

Jesus Is Filled With Pleasure

David mentions a third insight into the personality of the God-Man in Psalm 16:11. He says, "In Your presence is fullness of joy; at Your right hand are pleasures forevermore." I wrote a book on this subject called *The Pleasures of Loving God.* Let me make a few of those points here. As we have seen, David was a fanatic about the joy of God, the pleasure of God, and the gladness of God. He had a front-row seat into the happiness of God's heart. He said, "I drink from the river of Your pleasures, O God." (See Psalm 36:8.) David was using the language of poets to describe what it felt like when the Holy Spirit revealed God's emotions to him.

WE ARE HIS PRESENT DELIGHT. HE IS NOT WAITING FOR US TO ACHIEVE SOME LEVEL OF MATURITY OR SPIRITUAL STRENGTH.

Even more important than what David saw is how Peter, in Acts 2:28, interpreted this passage from the perspective of Jesus. In essence, Jesus is talking to the Father and says, "Father, You have made known to Me the ways of life. You will make Me full of joy in Your presence." What does it mean for the second Person of the Trinity to experience fullness of joy forever in the presence of His Father? It means that pleasure exists in the being and the personality of God. He is the Creator and originator of pleasure. Counterfeit pleasures only exist in the kingdom of darkness because Satan saw how effective and efficient they were as a motivator. But God is the Author of real pleasure. It springs from His very personality.

When God the Holy Spirit reveals the heart of God to the human spirit, it is the most exhilarating experience in this age and the age to come. It is the ultimate pleasure in created order. But that pleasure is not just for eternity; it's for this age as well. He gives us tokens of that pleasure now. He wants to motivate us, empower us, and protect us by letting us experience those pleasures as a down payment for what's coming. That strong pleasure turns to strong motivation. When the enemy comes to accuse God in my presence, I latch on to what I know to be true. I remind him, "It is written, 'His heart rejoices, His tongue is glad.' Even in my weakness, He is filled with joy when He looks at me." The enemy tries to tell me I'm a hopeless hypocrite, that Christianity is not working for me, and that I am uniquely messed up compared to everybody else. These are the same old lies he tells everybody. I respond with what is written in the Word about His rejoicing heart and His glad tongue. As high as the heavens are above the earth, that's how much He loves me (Isa. 55:8–9). I speak these words of God against the attack of the enemy and fill my heart and mind with truth.

Transformed by Jesus' Gladness

Beloved, you may not have experienced much of that exceeding joy we have been talking about. But God wants you to have it in your everyday life. There is so much more gladness God wants to bestow on you and me. The burden of my heart is that you won't wait until that final day to enter into Jesus' gladness. He does not *become* glad when you die; He is glad *now*. He was glad billions of years ago. He has been glad forever. It's who He is and what He does.

Yet I'm pained in my heart that the vast majority of the body of Christ still holds the view of a mostly mad or mostly sad God. Accusations and slander are lodged in their hearts against Him. People in the kingdom are nearly as depressed and filled with pain and complaint as people outside the kingdom. The Lord is not upset about this, but He would have us know that we are living in error. We are His present delight. He is not waiting for us to achieve some level of maturity or spiritual strength. I know from experience that it's impossible to talk people out of their misery.

Preaching and exhorting alone won't work. A rebuke won't stop their complaining, and a threat won't break their depression. We can speak on crankiness and despair all day long, and people will stay in the same place. We can only replace complaining with *experiencing God's joy.* As I mentioned in the last chapter, "happy holiness" speaks of a transformed heart of obedience that is the overflow of encountering the gladness of God's heart. We become glad with His gladness, and this energizes our life of holiness. This only comes as the gladness and joy of God's heart are revealed to you and to me and to others. Then people will touch reality as it flows from our lives.

You may hunger for this transformation in your own life, and that's wonderful. It's important to understand that the process is like peeling an onion with many layers. Our perception of God will not suddenly transform by reading a couple of Bible verses or books like this one. That moves us in the right direction, but we renew our minds by filling them continually with what God looks like and the truth of His heart. It's often mundane work, but you must fill your mind over and over with the truth from the Word of God. God designed us to learn gradually, over time, and so we are transformed by a thousand small instances of filling our minds with truth rather than one thunderbolt experience.

That process will yield major changes in you and me over time. In turn, it will change the way the church does God's business. And on the final day, we will stand before the throne, and affection will surge through our beings. We will be near the throne of God, which is surrounded with great joy. The King's heart will be full of gladness on the day of His wedding (Song of Sol. 3:11). This is a very real day in our future. We will smile and say, "This is incredible! I pictured this being a great day, but this goes way beyond my expectations." We will be glad because He is glad. We will rejoice because He is rejoicing. We will be stunned at the Father's kindness, at the possibility that such a river of pleasures exists. Beloved, this is where we are going. For eternity we will live in the wellspring of gladness. Yet it is not only for the age to come. He invites us to begin this celebration in this present age.

How do we do it? By beholding and becoming like our glad God. As we do this, we stop being scattered and ineffective, and instead we become people of "one thing." This is another major dimension of having a heart after God's, which we will study next.

Chapter Six

BECOMING A PERSON OF "ONE THING . . ."

For most of us, life presents dozens of options for career, lifestyle, passions, and hobbies. In our pursuit of pleasure and meaning we run here and there, trying one job or recreational activity after another, collecting experiences but never devoting ourselves to one direction. Christians do this in their spiritual lives and ministries as well, bouncing from one teaching or church to another, trying on ministries as they try on clothes. But today, the call of God to the church is to dismiss ourselves from chasing hither and thither and to cultivate a heart of unwavering devotion. He wants us to love Him, first and foremost, with all of our hearts. He wants us to be a people of one thing.

As you gaze upon the heart of God and begin to grasp that His emotions toward you are of gladness and burning passion for intimacy, nothing in the world will suffice. What you enjoy and desire narrows down to one thing. You begin to want to pour out your life in extravagant devotion upon the feet of Jesus. When your heart is conquered by the One who is fascinating, then no other captivation will satisfy. You will refuse to dwell anywhere but in this position of waiting on Him. You will pursue Him alone, not allowing yourself to be distracted by anything less. Your hunger will be fixed on a single source. There will be no going back to what used to bring satisfaction. Secondary pleasures will fade away.

Asking the Right Question

This way of living, while exhilarating, disturbs and provokes people who are still living for many things. They ask, "Why waste your time on that? Why this extreme devotion? What's going on here? You have to diversify, be more well-rounded, cultivate other interests. You're putting all your eggs in one basket." They don't understand the extravagance of being single-mindedly His. They feel blamed because their lifestyle is not focused on one thing. They might conclude that the person of one thing is mentally "off" or caught up in religious fanaticism, or that he or she has gone too far and will eventually swing back to normal.

TODAY, THE CALL OF GOD TO THE CHURCH IS TO DISMISS OURSELVES FROM CHASING HITHER AND THITHER AND TO CULTIVATE A HEART OF UNWAVERING DEVOTION.

But they misunderstand what's on the heart of God. The first commandment, the primary thing with which God is concerned, is, "Thou shalt love the Lord thy God with all thy heart, and with all thy soul, and with all thy mind" (Matt. 22:37, KJV). That is precisely what the Holy Spirit is saying to the church worldwide. He is cultivating hearts that are unreserved. He is promoting the kind of single-minded devotion the world is frightened of. Many in the church will reject it, and many will embrace it, but when the transformation is complete we will no longer ask, "What is the minimum that is required of me? What can I get by with?" Rather, we will ask, "What is the very most I can give? I want to give it all!" When you discover the pleasure of living for one thing, you become ruined for anything less.

A Costly Offering

The Bible gives compelling illustrations of extravagant devotion we can use as models for becoming people of one thing. The first picture is in 2 Samuel 23 when three of David's mighty men performed an amazing feat on behalf of their king.

> Then three of the thirty chief men . . . came to David at the cave of Adullum. . . . And David said with longing, "Oh, that someone would give me a drink of the water from the well of Bethlehem, which is by the gate!"
>
> —2 SAMUEL 23:13–15

At this time, David had been anointed king, but he was not king yet. Jealous King Saul was chasing him from cave to cave. In fleeing this evil pursuit, David wandered in the wilderness for about seven years as approximately three thousand men searched for him to kill him. About six hundred men joined David, and they made the cave of Adullum their main headquarters. The Philistines were defeating the nation of Israel and had just captured David's hometown, Bethlehem. It was probably late one night, and David was likely bemoaning the fact that the Philistines were moving in and taking so much of the land. I can imagine him and his men around the fire, the firelight and shadows dancing across their faces, and David saying with longing, "Oh, that someone would give me a drink of the water from the well of Bethlehem, which is by the gate!"

Some of the mighty warriors of David's army were at the front of the cave, no doubt guarding it from attack. Hearing David's longing, they got together and said, "Let's go get him some of that water." They knew it might cost them their lives, but they loved David with extravagance, and it thrilled their hearts to answer his request. They were a picture of the passionate loyalty we should have to Christ Jesus. They went far beyond the call of duty to answer the longing in their king's heart.

Three of David's mighty men gathered their swords and spears and went out. Undoubtedly as they approached the Philistine front line, they saw hundreds of enemy soldiers. Perhaps they were afraid for a moment, but that fear was overcome by the anticipation of that moment when they would bring their king what he desired, and so these mighty men broke through the Philistine camp and went all the way through the front line. I picture them working their way to the well and fighting for every inch of ground. Two of them probably fought while one scooped up the water. Once they retrieved it, they started back through the enemy line toward the cave of Adullum. I imagine them hissing to each other, "Don't spill that water, whatever you do! It's precious stuff." When they got back to the cave, they presented the water to David and proudly proclaimed, "We have the very water from the well of Bethlehem."

THE HOLY SPIRIT IS PROMOTING THE KIND OF SINGLE-MINDED DEVOTION THE WORLD IS FRIGHTENED OF.

David's eyes probably grew wide. I can imagine the appreciation, the thirst, the amazement he was feeling. But he would not drink the water he so desired because of its preciousness. He said, "Far be it from me, O LORD, that I should do this! Is this not the blood of the men who went in jeopardy of their lives?" (v. 17). He recognized that the water could have cost his men everything. He might have looked them square in the eye and said, "Your children could have been orphans. Your wives could have been widowed. You could have lost everything to get me this water. It's too holy for a man to drink because it represents your entire life." So David took the water and went before the Lord. The water was one of the most holy gifts that had ever been given to him, and he poured it out to the Lord and worshiped God with words that probably expressed this idea: "Father, only You are worthy of this water."

Of all the stories that could have been told of David and his men, this story became famous as one of the most extravagant acts of devotion toward the king. There were 1.3 million soldiers in David's army at the peak of his military career (2 Sam. 24:9). From that number, God highlighted only three examples of exceptional valor and commitment to David. It's important to pay attention to them. For us, this becomes a picture of devotion to King Jesus. It's a pattern for becoming people of one thing, with hearts after God's.

What made those men risk their lives for a few drinks of water? Was it boredom? Bluster? Misplaced bravery? Desire for fame? Desire for promotion? Did they want a pay raise from David or an easier schedule or some time off to spend with their families? I don't think so. I believe the courage of David's mighty men came from one thing: their absolute, to-the-death devotion to him. Their boldness and perseverance that spurred them to unusual feats of bravery sprang from sold-out commitment to David, representing for us the Lord Jesus. I imagine them answering to David for sneaking off to get the water. I can almost hear them say, "David, we didn't care about losing our lives. Don't you see? We lost our lives when we joined you."

David was a symbol of their salvation. When these mighty

men came to him, they were distressed, discontented, and in debt, and David became their captain. The crowd that gathered to him in the cave of Adullum was the most motley youth group in the history of Israel. David redeemed them from worthless lives. When they had nothing to live for, he gave them a vision and a cause. He trained them and made them an army and a family. He shared his heart with them, and their hearts were ennobled and encouraged. They saw the beauty of who David was, his godliness, and the favor of God upon him. They became men of one thing, willing to live courageously because of their burning love for him. This illustrates exactly the kind of abandonment God wants us to give to Christ Jesus.

> I BELIEVE THE COURAGE OF DAVID'S MIGHTY MEN CAME FROM ONE THING: THEIR ABSOLUTE, TO-THE-DEATH DEVOTION TO HIM.

Beloved, we will have the courage to do extravagant acts of valor only when our hearts are enraptured by our God. The Lord desires people who go beyond the minimum requirements. He searches for lives of lavish commitment. Our goal should be to stand before Him on the last day and offer ourselves to Him just as these three men offered the water to David at the expense of their lives. Paul said in 1 Corinthians 15:28 that on the last day Jesus will gather all these sweet things called the devotion of His people and place it at His Father's feet. Then He will kneel down and offer Himself to His Father so that His Father will be all in all. In that moment we will be Jesus' gift back to His Father. We will be the sweet water He offers. This prophetic picture will be complete. He will take us and pour us out to God the Father, just as David poured out the water from the well of Bethlehem.

That is the bride's heart. It seeks to give more to the Bridegroom—more time, more money, and more passion. We want to do whatever He will empower the human heart to do. Things we didn't think we could accomplish come into the realm of possibility when the heart is willing. We must ask the Lord how deep we can go into the very center of extravagance. We must pursue Him and ask permission to do acts of great valor and courage for Him. That is the spirit of the bride, and it resided in the hearts of David's mighty men. They heard the whisper of their king's desires, and they risked their lives to bring him his heart's desire.

For the Prize of Knowing Him

> But what things were gain to me, these I have counted loss for Christ. Yet indeed I also count all things loss for the excellence of the knowledge of Christ Jesus my Lord, for whom I have suffered the loss of all things, and count them as rubbish, that I might gain Christ... that I may know Him and the power of His resurrection, and the fellowship of His sufferings, being conformed to His death.
>
> —PHILIPPIANS 3:7–8, 10

Our second illustration of being people of one thing comes from Philippians 3, where Paul gave an autobiographical look at what motivated him. He sometimes gave a sentence here and there in his other writings, but I don't know any place where he shared his deepest heart so richly. Without apology, Paul pointed us to the necessity of *fierce abandonment* for the sake of one thing. He confirmed that stunning and fascinating things happen when new discoveries of the God-Man touch our spirit. Verse 8 says, "Oh the excellencies of knowing Christ Jesus my Lord, for whom I have suffered the loss of all things! I count all of these losses as rubbish that

I may experience Him" (author's paraphrase). Paul was not saying that he suffered these things to earn Jesus' approval, but that in forsaking them, he removed what hindered his ability to experience Jesus to the fullest possible degree. He purposely narrowed his options. He willingly became a man of one thing.

In verse 10, Paul gave three foundations of his inner motivation. By the anointing of the Holy Spirit, he put them together in a strategic way.

1. "I want to know Him," speaking of sharing intimacy with Jesus.
2. "I want to know the power of His resurrection," speaking of the ability to operate in the anointing.
3. "I want to know the fellowship of His sufferings," portraying his desire to bear the inevitable counterattack of suffering and persecution.

Paul understood the paradox that even as the anointing prepares and equips the heart for suffering, it also triggers the counterattack that brings suffering. It starts a chain reaction in the kingdom of darkness. When we operate in new levels of the anointing and plunder Satan's kingdom, we touch new dimensions of counterattack. Paul actually gloried in the privilege of having intimacy with Jesus in suffering, which is a necessary dimension of the kingdom of God.

In verse 12, Paul revealed the inner activity of his soul: "I press on." In other words, he committed himself to experiencing the three things he spoke of in verse 10. He said, "I want to lay hold of that for which I was laid hold of by God." The Lord Jesus laid hold of each one of us for a very specific reason. God had something in mind for you when you were born and when you were born again. You were "laid hold of by God," handpicked by Him in His creative genius and created with certain passions. But it is so common in the kingdom of God today for people to never lay hold of the thing for which they were born and to never enter into the destiny God prepared for them. This is because we are not yet a people of one thing. We are not people after His heart. We are trying to do business as usual. We don't want fellow Christians to think we're strange; we don't want discomfort. We want to live as everybody else lives. But we're in danger of not laying hold of what God has for us in this hour of history.

THE LORD DESIRES PEOPLE WHO GO BEYOND THE MINIMUM REQUIREMENTS.

Paul went on to say that he didn't consider himself to have already attained to this. He didn't believe he had fully apprehended the fullness of what he was created for. Yet he committed himself to one thing: to forget the things that were behind him and press on to what was ahead. Paul was a single-minded man, much as David was. He reached forward to take hold of knowing Christ, of experiencing the power of His resurrection and the fellowship of His suffering. He determined in his heart to spend his entire life doing this. He went out of his way to remove any known hindrances to his destiny in God.

Beloved, we will not accidentally lay hold of the highest things God has called us to. We must press into them knowing that the devil will press back. We must push against our resisting flesh. We must fight as believers and unbelievers alike come against us. We must lay hold of the prize, and the only way to accomplish that is by being individuals and churches of extravagant devotion to Jesus. No other kind of devotion will survive the onslaught of the enemy.

I believe that the "prize" Paul referenced in verse 14 was the experience of intimacy and power spoken of in verse 10. He wanted the dimension of power and fellowship that was found only in suffering for the gospel. His prize was not just eternal, but it was meant to be experienced in some measure on Earth. Daniel prophesied about this same reality saying, "The people who know their God shall be strong, and carry out great exploits....Yet for many days they shall fall by sword and flame, by captivity and plundering" (Dan. 11:32–33). Daniel spoke of two different time periods in this prophecy. First was the time of Antiochus in 175–167 B.C., which was a type of persecution just before the Second Coming of Jesus. The second time frame is at the end of the age. This tells us the people of God will know their God, will have a mighty spirit, and will do great exploits. They will also know suffering and will fall by the sword and flame as martyrs. Notice that Daniel described the same three things Paul described, these three dimensions of being a people of one thing:

> WE MUST LAY HOLD OF THE PRIZE, AND THE ONLY WAY TO ACCOMPLISH THAT IS BY BEING INDIVIDUALS AND CHURCHES OF EXTRAVAGANT DEVOTION TO JESUS.

1. Knowing God
2. Operating in the anointing
3. Being equipped to fellowship with Him in suffering

In this pursuit, we must not apologize for our intensity. We must not accept some idea of "balance" that is not the balance of the Spirit, though it might be the balance of religious man. We want to be balanced Jesus-style, so that God says on the last day,

"You had a fiery heart. You bore the sufferings. You learned to operate in the anointing. You knew how to worship in the Spirit. You were a person of one thing, after My own heart." That is balance from God's point of view.

What's the point of being a person of one thing? What do we gain? God Himself! God revealed Himself as the primary reward of the human heart in Genesis 15:1 when He stood before Abraham and said, "Do not be afraid, Abram. I am your shield, your exceedingly great reward." Those words amaze me. God reveals Himself as our prize. He is the ultimate satisfaction of our hearts. He gives us secondary rewards, too, and I love them as well. There's the anointing to touch the ends of the earth. There's health, wealth, influence, anointed ministry, and favor in significant relationships. God gave all of these to Abraham and promised them to us. But they are all secondary. *God Himself* was the great reward surpassing all others. He is the prize of the ages.

God demonstrated this truth again with the story of Levi.

> At that time the LORD separated the tribe of Levi *to bear the ark of the covenant* of the LORD, to stand before the LORD to minister to Him and to bless in His name, to this day. Therefore Levi has no portion nor inheritance with his brethren; the LORD is his inheritance, just as the LORD your God promised him.
>
> —DEUTERONOMY 10:8–9, EMPHASIS ADDED

In this passage, the phrase "to bear the ark of the covenant" symbolized receiving the presence of God. God separated the tribe of Levi to bear the ark, or to experience the presence of the Lord. He set them apart to stand before Him and bless the name of God. That was their anointing. Because of this unique blessing, Levi and his brothers received no portion of the land and no inheritance when the other tribes of Israel received their portion.

Why? Because the Lord Himself was Levi's inheritance. "The LORD is their inheritance" (Deut. 18:2). God set this tribe apart to receive the greatest blessing: the reward and the inheritance of Himself. That's a picture of true intimacy with God, when we don't need anything else but Him to make our lives complete.

Beloved, this prize will not automatically fall at our feet. There is a pressing in. We reach for the one thing, the exceedingly great reward. There is a forgetting of what came before, both success and failure. In Philippians 3:13 Paul said, "One thing I do, forgetting those things which are behind." Part of our offering to the Lord is forgetting our dedication and personal sacrifice. Paul counted them as nothing. We do not stand before the Lord and calculate how much we have given Him in prayer, fasting, finances, and persecution. We forget all that because our glory is not found in anything we can give. Our glory is in being loved by Him and in the anointing to love Him. That alone gives us value. When we become preoccupied with our sacrifice, religious pride steals in, and our motives become corrupt.

GOD HIMSELF WAS THE GREAT REWARD SURPASSING ALL OTHERS. HE IS THE PRIZE OF THE AGES.

We also should forget our accomplishments. God doesn't look at spiritual résumés. The great revivals we lead, the Bible schools we started, the ministries we ran—these are not our offering. No matter how many people we lead to the Lord or how many sermons we preach or how many people grow to spiritual maturity under our leadership, these mean nothing when compared to the privilege of knowing Christ. We should discount them, let them go. God will reckon them in proper balance when we get to heaven, but for us there is nothing so valuable as simply knowing God.

For this reason we should also let our failures go. These can distract us more than our accomplishments. Paul tells us to forget all these things and press in to God's heart with a spiritual violence, reaching toward the prize with all the energy we have. That's how we want to live. We want to be a people of one thing, forgetting what is behind and pressing to what is ahead. That's how we become men and women after God's own heart.

Lovesick Worshipers

One of the greatest examples of a lifestyle of one thing is Mary of Bethany. She's one of my favorite people in the Gospels, and in the next chapter I want to show how her life, like David's, teaches us to be men and women after God's own heart.

Chapter Seven

MARY OF BETHANY: A WOMAN OF "ONE THING . . ."

Have you wondered where you would go and what you would do if you had just a few days to live? Which people would you want around you? How would you plan your schedule? Jesus faced such questions the week before He was crucified. He could spend His last days with whomever He chose, so He went to the small town of Bethany where Lazarus, whom He had raised from the dead, and his two sisters, Mary and Martha, lived.

Why Bethany? Why Lazarus, Mary, and Martha? Why not go hang out with Joseph of Arimathea, a powerful and wealthy man? He probably had a nice home with all the comforts of the day. Why not relax and rest up for the tough days to come? Or how about Nicodemus, a religious leader? Why not sow into learned, powerful men like him? Or why not spend time in the wilderness with His disciples, getting in some last-minute teaching? Because none of these people loved and understood His heart as Mary, Martha, and Lazarus did. Undoubtedly, Jesus was filled with many wrenching thoughts and emotions about the approaching days. He had resolutely set His face to Jerusalem to offer Himself as the debt payment for all humanity. He had shared this with the disciples, but they hadn't grasped it. So He went to people who loved the heart of God, who understood something about Jesus that most others didn't. They were His best friends. The Bible tells us Jesus deeply loved Mary, Martha, and Lazarus (John 11:5). He loved everybody, but He had a special friendship with them.

Mary in particular loved Him extravagantly. She knew He was going to die very soon, and she had it in her heart to pour out abundant love on Jesus before He was crucified. She had decided, as she mulled it over during her chores and other day-to-day tasks, that she would give an unthinkable love offering. She would anoint Him for burial with her own inheritance. Knowing that He was about to give His life—an extravagant gift unmatched in all history—she determined to give all that she had as a suitable response (Mark 14:8). Thus she set her heart to anoint Him with expensive perfume. I believe it was not a spur-of-the-moment idea but a deliberate action she had pondered for some time in the recesses of her heart. It was a deed born of understanding and revelation. It was a beautiful flower that would bloom in those troubled times.

THEY SAW WASTE, NEEDLESS SQUANDERING. BUT JESUS SAW THE ETERNAL SIGNIFICANCE AND SILENCED THEM.

Her moment came when all were gathered at Simon the leper's house for a supper prepared in Jesus' honor. Perhaps Martha was serving the group of about seventeen men who were gathered. Her brother Lazarus probably reclined at the table with Jesus. The scene was set. Suddenly and with great boldness, Mary burst into the room clutching an alabaster vial of perfume. She felt passionate about what she was going to do. Her heart was ablaze. Martha and Lazarus immediately recognized what she carried. This bottle was her inheritance, filled with the most costly perfume in all of Palestine, worth a year's wages. It was her entire life savings and her only financial stability for the future. Without warning and without a word, she rushed into the room, broke open the precious bottle, and poured it on Jesus' head. The perfumed oil flowed down His head to His feet, and Mary fell to her knees. Lovingly, she began to soak her hair in the perfume and wash Jesus' feet with it. Her entire inheritance was gone in a moment.

Immediately, the powerful fragrance permeated the house (John 12:3). Martha came out of the kitchen with a gasp. Everyone in the room fell utterly silent, and their eyes widened. As it dawned on them what she had done, many of them grew angry and offended. "But there were some who were indignant among themselves, and said, 'Why was this fragrant oil wasted?'" (Mark 14:4). I can hear Martha saying, "There she goes again. Lord, look what she's done now!" As with any extravagant act, it provoked controversy. The disciples argued that the perfume could have been sold and the money given to the poor. They saw waste, needless squandering, because they saw with the eyes of the flesh.

But Jesus saw the eternal significance and silenced them. "Let her alone. Why do you trouble her? She has done a good work for Me" (v. 6). He was saying, "Don't you understand? I'm going to die. The poor will be here a week from now, but I will not. Mary has done all that she could in showing lavish devotion to Me. She anointed My body beforehand for burial. This is not about economics. This is about a woman's heart who understands the prophetic hour that I'm in."

> Assuredly, I say to you, wherever this gospel is preached in the whole world, what this woman has

done will also be told as a memorial to her.

—Mark 14:9

Jesus could have rightly added, "Bartholomew, people will never remember who you were. Andrew, they won't know much about you. Most of you will get little ink in the Gospels. Yet you can be sure that the nations of the world will know about Mary." I imagine her friends asked her afterward, "Mary, what about tomorrow? What will you do? You had such a good future ahead, but you wasted your inheritance." I believe her heart would have responded, "I have Him. *He* is my tomorrow."

THE KEY TO SUSTAINING OUR INTENSE DESIRE TO BE FULLY GIVEN TO GOD IS TO HAVE FRESH ENCOUNTERS WITH HIS HEART.

It has been said that all of church history has been filled with the fragrance of this woman's deed. The Lord established her life and this one moment as a picture of God's delight in our extravagant devotion. She did not have all of the sovereign appointments of an apostle, yet she had the same quality of the heart and the same success as an apostle in the eyes of God. Jesus affirmed that Mary understood the one necessary thing that life is about (Luke 10:38–42).

In our day, the Holy Spirit is emphasizing the anointing that was upon Mary of Bethany, which is the anointing to "waste" our lives on one thing: extravagant devotion to Jesus Christ. It is the anointing to linger long with an engaged spirit in the presence of the Lord. This is impossible to do with religious self-determination and the power of the flesh. We can't will ourselves to be more resolute and say, "I will, I will, I will." The abandonment flows out of a lovesick heart.

Intimacy Sustains Our Intensity

Mary of Bethany, Abraham, the apostle Paul, and David's mighty men all found the secret of a focused life. They tapped into the glory and pleasure of giving themselves to *one thing.* God invites each of us to do the same and to give ourselves wholeheartedly to Him. We can stand with these so-called giants of the faith. We can touch the same flame that caused them to say, "I count all things loss for the excellence of knowing this Man, Christ Jesus!" (See Philippians 3:8.)

The key to sustaining our intense desire to be fully given to God is to have fresh encounters with His heart. I have seen many people at conferences or meetings respond fully to the message to be radical, wholehearted followers of Jesus. However, the call to be wholehearted is not the same as the ability to walk it out day to day.

What is needed? We must equip or train our hearts to actually walk out the wholeheartedness that we so intensely desire. This equipping of the heart is best found in intimacy. Our intense desire to be radical for God will be sustained with regular experiences of God's heart.

The most important principle that you can get from this book is the truth that has been proven over and over throughout church history—*intimacy sustains intensity.*

We can be people after God's own heart!

A Heart of Devotion

Mary of Bethany's example jumps out at me from Scripture because she had nothing to set her apart from the many other followers of Jesus but a heart of devotion. She was a young, single woman with no distinctive leadership gifts and no public ministry. She had no special gifting or calling, and she experienced no angelic visitations that we know of. All that Scripture reveals to us is her devotion. Her life is remembered as *the* life that moved God.

She was the only woman whom the Lord openly honored (Mark 14:9), just as John the Baptist was the only man (John 5:35).

> Now it happened as they went that He entered a certain village; and a certain woman named Martha welcomed Him into her house. And she had a sister called Mary, who also sat at Jesus' feet and heard His word.
> —LUKE 10:38–39

Mary appeared three times in Scripture, in three different episodes of life, and on each occasion she was sitting at the feet of Jesus (Luke 10:39; John 11:32; 12:3). This was no accident of writing or editing. The Holy Spirit expressly emphasized this as her way of life. She was always there when Jesus was around, listening and pouring her love out to Him. She was much more than a groupie who hangs around for the thrill of being near a celebrity. She was, rather, someone who could peer into the Savior's heart more clearly than most and understand His emotions. Others followed Jesus for the power or the teaching or the excitement of the crowd, but Mary didn't care for those things. She cared about the emotional connection. And so, when Jesus came, she let other responsibilities go and prized every minute in His presence. And at the same time, she was always criticized for it. Every time she appeared in the Bible, she was bearing the brunt of someone's harsh words, yet she was never described as giving an answer to defend herself. She had developed this rare quality by living before an audience of One.

JOYFUL INTIMACY WITH GOD IS THE GREAT POWER SOURCE OF THE KINGDOM OF GOD.

In Luke 10:42, Jesus said, "But one thing is needed, and Mary has chosen that good part, which will not be taken away from her." Mary had one cause beating in her heart, and nobody could pull it away from her. This "one thing" is not the only thing in the kingdom of God. Jesus did not say, "There is only one thing that you will do in the Christian life." Rather, He pointed to Mary's heart of devotion and said that such a gazing heart is all you need to focus on; the rest will flow from that. Joyful intimacy with God is the great power source of the kingdom of God. It's the means by which the Holy Spirit continually supplies the heart with power. In essence, Jesus was saying, "When the human heart is engaged with God in intimacy and devotion in these ways, then I assure you that the rest of the major things of the kingdom will happen in their time." The gazing heart of devotion is the primary thing that sets everything else in motion in the divine order.

Mary gave herself to what Jesus called the first commandment: loving the Lord her God with all her heart, soul, and mind (Matt. 22:37). The first commandment must be first, and the second commandment must be second. The first commandment has to do with a gazing heart that learns, enjoys, and becomes a wholehearted lover of God. The second tells us to love our neighbor as ourselves. If our hearts don't first encounter the fire of His heart, we will sooner or later burn out in loving others.

Maybe you have known people who approach their ministry with spunk and a can-do attitude, but after a while their eyes dim, they sit in their office behind closed doors, and the joy seems to have leaked out of them like a flat tire. Most likely, they switched the order of the commandments. When the second commandment is put in first place, there is not enough energy to carry out the task of loving our neighbor, and so ministry flounders. Worse, the church becomes an idol that hinders the kingdom of God.

It may seem "wasteful," but there is no safer place, no more powerful place than sitting at the feet of Jesus and becoming experts on the first commandment—learning to love God with all our hearts, souls, and minds. There at His feet we are empowered and equipped to fulfill the second commandment and do kingdom works. We don't run out of energy by Thursday afternoon. We're not edgy and brittle with people when we feel tired. If we get the first commandment right, the second will flow naturally from it. We don't need to worry about someone who wants to sit at the feet of Jesus for long hours. We don't need to fret that they are "off balance." It is a false argument that one must choose between the first and second commandments. Anyone who sits at the feet of Jesus, given a little bit of time, will run headlong into the great Evangelist and His kindness and compassion. The first commandment is the very foundation of soul-winning power. People like Mary of Bethany inevitably develop a burning heart like His for people. When the first commandment is in first place, the second commandment is energized.

YOU MAY HAVE ALREADY GUESSED THAT ALL THE POWERS OF HELL WILL FIGHT TO KEEP US FROM BEING A PEOPLE OF ONE THING.

We see in Martha's criticism the worry and irritability that come from out-of-place priorities, which undermine our ability to enjoy intimacy with God. Martha's opinions became too important in her own eyes. Minor things became majors. She was easily frustrated and couldn't engage her spirit with God. She had stifled the free-flowing heart of devotion that Mary had preserved.

You may have already guessed that all the powers of hell will fight to keep us from being a people of one thing. They work to get our options out of order, keeping us busy with everything but learning to love God. In the Western world, both inside and outside the church, we suffer from option fatigue. Hundreds of options present themselves to us from the moment we wake up to the moment we go to bed, and even in our dreams at night. We think of going to the mall, planning a vacation, visiting an amusement park, going to the lake, fixing the screen in the bathroom, watching a new TV show, going to a new restaurant, reading a magazine, calling a friend... and the list goes on forever. We cultivate the superficial appetites of Western culture and fail to develop deep hunger for any one thing. We nibble on so many meaningless things that our hunger for meaningful things gets lost like a single piece of confetti in a ticker-tape parade. Just as Martha fought to convince Mary she was supposed to do something other than be with Jesus, our consciences nag us to do a hundred things that are not the will of God for our lives. We are full of other things and so feel no hunger, but we're dying of spiritual malnutrition.

The enemy has been terribly successful at distracting us. It is highly unusual to come across a person leading a lifestyle of devotion. God has called us to keep the first thing first, and from that, all the secondary things will flow. He is making plain the one necessary "option" of gazing on Him and sitting at His feet. From this focused lifestyle, everything else will flow. We have to learn to rest in that truth.

Deep Trust in Time of Crisis

When we become people of one thing, we are not easily offended by the Lord, as many Christians are today. We are not quickly alienated by distrust for His motives.

> Now a certain man was sick, Lazarus of Bethany, the town of Mary and her sister Martha.... Lazarus was sick. Therefore the sisters sent to Him, saying, "Lord, behold, he whom You love is sick." When Jesus heard that, He said, "This sickness is not unto death, but for

> the glory of God. . . ." Now Jesus loved Martha and her sister and Lazarus.
>
> —John 11:1–5

In this chapter we see Mary's trust in a time of crisis and her resignation to the Lord's leadership. Her heart was free from offense toward Jesus for not healing Lazarus. What a tough lesson to swallow, especially in the days immediately following Lazarus' death. Yet she trusted His leadership though He hadn't come at her request in time to heal him. When Jesus arrived at Bethany, Martha was at the grave site taking charge of the situation, and Mary was at home weeping. Jesus sent for her, and she quickly arose and went to meet Him. When she saw Him, she fell at His feet and began to weep, but she was not angry with Him. She acknowledged Him as Lord and declared that His power was sufficient. "Lord, if You had been here, my brother would not have died" (v. 32).

Have you ever watched a loved one weep? Have you seen his or her eyes well up and spill over with tears and pain that could no longer be contained? A person's entire countenance changes as it becomes red and swollen with grief. There is no hiding your heart when you weep; it is all laid out on the table. But as you watch a spouse or child, brother or sister in that moment of pain, your heart leaps out of you, and you wish you could share that burden. You probably feel as Jesus did. "Therefore, when Jesus saw her weeping. . . He groaned in the spirit and was troubled" (v. 33). Jesus wept not because of Mary's unbelief; He wept because His heart had the same reaction yours and mine would. His best friend was hurting; it was written all over her face in vivid colors. She couldn't even hide her sadness, and here she was on the ground before Him, still trusting Him through it all.

Mary's moment of pain was good enough reason for Jesus to weep. We have no other recorded theological reason for why Jesus wept, only the reason of intimacy and friendship. Mary's pain moved Jesus in His humanity. Though He knew He was going to heal Lazarus in just a moment, He saw that Mary was brokenhearted. His response reveals how deeply He was impacted by the movements of her heart. He knew she would carry some of the pain of His heart at the time of His death. But Mary didn't become offended. She trusted Him in her moment of deepest crisis. Her heart had been shaped in those times of sitting at His feet to trust Him implicitly, because she knew the goodness of His heart.

By being people of one thing, we help to immunize our hearts against that sense of betrayal the enemy would like us to buy into. He brings us a list of grievances and encourages us to confront God with them, as if that were possible. He wants us to step away from that intrinsic trust we have in Him and begin to see Him as our adversary. He wants us to blame God when things don't go the way we envision. But, like Mary, we can know Him well enough to trust Him in the time of deepest crisis. And even in those hard moments when we lack understanding, He will share the emotions of our heart, weeping with us even as He brings us toward a miracle.

THE PERSON LIVING FOR ONE THING MAY NEVER SPEAK A WORD, BUT HIS OR HER LIFESTYLE WILL BECOME A TOUCHSTONE, A DIVIDING LINE.

Why This Waste?

But the disciples' question echoes through the ages and is repeated by many if not most in the church today: "Why this waste?" The lifestyle of one thing, exemplified by intimacy with God, is considered inefficient and disruptive. Many study and teach on this lifestyle from the pulpit and in the classroom, but when someone actually lives it, he or she is labeled a fanatic. The idea preaches well, but it doesn't fit in "normal" Christian circles when it's lived out.

Though it may not be popular, the lifestyle of one thing is biblical, orthodox, good, and right. Nobody has to apologize for living intensely before God. Nobody has to make excuses for doing more than what is *required* and offering Him wholehearted love. In our day God is cultivating this heart of unwavering devotion in people across the earth. This is polarizing different groups in the church. Those who embrace one thing can expect to hear increasing cries of, "Why this waste?" There will be upheaval in religious organizations as extravagant devotion provokes harsh reactions, even incriminations. The person living for one thing may never speak a word, but his or her lifestyle will become a touchstone, a dividing line. Observers will have to decide if such a lifestyle is right or wrong. They will have to decide if they too will pour out their entire earthly life span, their inheritance, as an offering to Him as Mary did.

But once you discover the *superior pleasure* of God, there is no going back. You taste and see that the Lord is good (Ps. 34:8). You whittle your life down to one thing, and, as the Lord said to Mary, it will not be taken from you. When we ask Him for the grace to lead lives of total abandonment, we start on the path of contending for the fullness of God's power. Like David and Mary of Bethany, we become ruined for anything less than the highest God wants to give us. That's our direction in the next chapter, where we'll talk about contending for the power of God in our generation.

Chapter Eight

CONTENDING FOR THE POWER OF GOD

We looked in the beginning at David's passion for obeying the commands of God's heart. He said, "I delight to do Your will, O my God, and Your law [Word] is within my heart" (Ps. 40:8). We also discussed his unmatched example as a student of the emotions of God's heart. He proclaimed, "One thing I have desired of the LORD . . . to behold the beauty of the LORD" (Ps. 27:4). Now I want to look at a third expression of what it means to be a person after God's heart: *contending for the fullness of God's power and purpose in our generation.*

First, we should recognize that the complete fullness of God, as it is manifested in eternity, is beyond anything we can imagine in this age. That is not what I mean by "fullness." But in every hour of history there are divine strategies and measures of grace that God chooses to release for that particular time. There is a "fullness" for each generation. That's the fullness of which I'm speaking.

Second, we should recognize that the fullness of God's purpose will look different for each generation. For example, King David did not have the same opportunity to operate in the anointing to do miracles as the apostle Paul did in the Book of Acts. Paul didn't have the anointing to accomplish supernatural military feats as David did. Our job is to press into the fullness of whatever God is offering His people in the season of history we live in. We should be like David, who "served the purpose of God in his own generation" (Acts 13:36, NAS). We should ask, "Lord, how much of Your power will You give us? What more do You have planned for us? What's the highest and most and best we can do for You?"

Contending for Apostolic Power

I believe we are in the generation in which Jesus will return, which means we have the opportunity to experience the power of God that surpasses even what is written about in the Book of Acts. We have much to contend for. But what does it mean to *contend* for the fullness of God? Simply this: to work against the obstacles that keep God's purpose from being manifested in our generation. It means refusing to back down until the power of God breaks out in full revival. It means doing everything God has in mind to heal the sick, deliver the demonized, and draw the unbeliever to saving faith through lifestyles of prayer, fasting, happy holiness, and wholeheartedness for God. Jude gave a strong exhortation, saying:

> Beloved...I found it necessary to write to you exhorting you to contend earnestly for the faith which was once for all delivered to the saints.
>
> —Jude 3

Jude was saying we must fight for the apostolic faith and power of New Testament Christianity that was delivered to us by the apostles and to the apostles by the Lord Jesus Himself. Notice

Jude said "once for all," meaning this apostolic faith should be a hallmark of Christianity at all times of history. The power of God never gets out of date or goes out of style.

What is the apostolic faith we're talking about? There are three facets to it:

1. Proclamation of apostolic doctrine
2. Demonstration of apostolic power
3. Living holy lifestyles of simplicity and abandonment to God, which includes fasting

Typically, Christians in our day limit the meaning of "contending for faith" to fighting for sound doctrine. That's not altogether wrong. The proclamation of apostolic truth is vital, and we all should commit to it. But there is more to the apostolic faith than just doctrine. It has a *power dimension* that we see manifested so clearly in the Book of Acts and throughout the New Testament. This dimension is inseparable from the other facets of the faith. Unfortunately, many teachers ignore this aspect of the faith because it doesn't fit their preferred theology or because they are afraid of it.

Our job is to press into the fullness of whatever God is offering His people in the season of history we live in.

Suppose a Christian man from the twenty-first century met the apostle Paul and told him he wanted sound doctrine, but he wasn't interested in healing the sick and casting out demons. I'm sure Paul would correct him and say, "Wait a second. If you only have the right dogma but don't demonstrate the power of it, you won't fully live out apostolic faith." As my friend Sam Storms, a professor at Wheaton College, likes to say, "We must know the power of truth and experience the truth about power." We must contend for biblical *experience* together with biblical ideas. It is not enough to have good doctrine with a clean life. That's only part of the equation. We must also have the power to deliver the oppressed and needy. By the same token, it's not sufficient to experience power in ministry while living in secret sin or espousing false doctrine. We need all three—lifestyles of radiant righteousness, sound doctrine, and the power of God to deliver the oppressed.

This is the apostolic faith that was once and for all delivered by Jesus and the apostles. This is the faith that we are contending for today.

Sadly, I observe a growing sentiment in the body of Christ against all three dimensions of apostolic faith. Some people prefer sound doctrine but don't care to cultivate the power of God for healing. Others enjoy the power ministry but don't care for holiness or sound doctrine. We must resist any tide of popularity that minimizes any aspect of the faith. Paul wrote:

> For the time will come when they will not endure sound doctrine, but according to their own desires, because they have itching ears, they will heap up for themselves teachers; and they will turn their ears away from the truth, and be turned aside to fables.
>
> —2 Timothy 4:3–4

In other words, the days are coming—in fact, I believe they are here—when people desire doctrine that suits their own preferences. Just like the passage about contending for the faith in Jude 3, the "sound doctrine" referred to in this verse is often interpreted as being limited to theology alone. Yes, sound doctrine includes understanding the truth of God's Word. But let me reiterate that there is no such thing as sound doctrine that does not have apostolic power and righteousness. Paul's prophecy is being fulfilled now in our nation. Professing believers are surrendering one or more of the three dimensions of apostolic faith, according to their religious tastes. Usually, of the three, people let go of biblical orthodoxy last. For some reason they hang on to truth long after they let go of power and godliness. Perhaps they think that if they can lay it out on paper right, all will be OK. Some of these professed believers may pastor large congregations where thousands gather and where ministry seems outwardly healthy and vibrant. My question is, is it a New Testament congregation or a collection of people with itching ears who want to be repeatedly assured that they'll be fine in lifestyles of powerless Christianity? Have our churches lost the apostolic faith handed down by the Lord?

WE NEED ALL THREE—LIFESTYLES OF RADIANT RIGHTEOUSNESS, SOUND DOCTRINE, AND THE POWER OF GOD TO DELIVER THE OPPRESSED.

Seeking God's Face and His Hand

There is a familiar saying that seems to be growing more popular, and it says we should seek God's face and not His hand. Seeking His face refers to intimacy, and seeking His hand speaks of God's blessings, including the release of His power in ministry. This saying sounds great, but it's not biblical. Scripture never instructs us to put intimacy with God in an adversarial relationship with God's power in ministry. They are not at odds. Rather, they are partners. We seek God's power to set the captives free so that they also might experience intimacy with Jesus.

The only truth within the phrase is that seeking God's face should be the first priority, and seeking power in ministry should be second. But we should resist any suggestion that seeking power is wrong. It is wrong when it becomes a higher priority than intimacy, but it is equally wrong to neglect seeking power at all. The apostle Paul exhorted us to "seek earnestly the greater gifts" (1 Cor. 12:31, NAS). We must fight until we regularly see Holy Spirit demonstrations of power to deliver the sick and oppressed so that the gospel might go forth in power as we evangelize. This dimension of contending for the faith is sorely lacking in the body of Christ. We desperately need a fresh release of apostolic power to cast demons out and heal the sick today! People are tired of sermons about yesterday's power. They are tired of reading about the way the gospel worked back then without seeing it at work now. Oh, the vast multitudes that would be saved if the power of apostolic faith went forth! Oh, the fame His name would gain among nations!

I believe that Acts 19:11 is more than a history lesson; I believe it is a vision statement from God's heart to us in this generation. It says, "God did extraordinary miracles through Paul" (NIV). Even handkerchiefs or aprons that were brought from his body to the sick caused the diseases and evil spirits to leave. Revival broke out in Ephesus, which was like a New York City of its day, and the fear of God fell upon it. The name of the Lord Jesus was magnified, and many who had believed came confessing their sins. Those who had practiced magic and the dark arts brought their magic books and burned them in sight of everybody. The Word of God grew mighty and prevailed over an entire major city in the earth. It reminds me of back in 1857, when Charles Finney had five hundred thousand converts in eight weeks in New York City. The Word of God was prevailing there. Beloved, that is the vision I have for the cities of the earth. I believe God is going to release unusual miracles by the hands of His servants. I believe people are going to have such a life in God that they will be known in hell itself.

One of the great problems of the hour in which we live is that a lot of people's vision starts and stops with having a popular ministry before men. The passion of many of God's servants is to be known on the earth. But Paul was known in hell, which means he had an authority that was known in the realm of the angels and the demons. These demons had no idea who the sons of Sceva were (Acts 19:14–15). They had never trembled at their prayer lives or preaching. But they had trembled at Paul's prayer life. I'm convinced that some reading this book will one day be known in hell because of the anointing on their lives. Demons didn't know Paul because he was famous as a teacher studying under Gamaliel. They only knew of him because of his life in God, and we have the same opportunity to lead that kind of life.

WE DESPERATELY NEED A FRESH RELEASE OF APOSTOLIC POWER TO CAST DEMONS OUT AND HEAL THE SICK TODAY! PEOPLE ARE TIRED OF SERMONS ABOUT YESTERDAY'S POWER.

The Lord is calling us right now to shift out of the common mode of Christian ministry into a lifestyle of apostolic, New Testament power. I have a vision for what Paul called the perfected power being released, not just the introductory dimensions of power. I want to see unusual miracles, demons backing away through the prayers of the saints. I believe it is happening to a point, but nothing compared to the kind of authority God wants to release to His children. There is a difference between the introductory grace and anointing of God that come to us at salvation and the greater realms that God gives those who take the kingdom by force, who press in to His heart with a vision for the fullness of God's power. The introductory dimensions are automatic. All you do is show up and say, "Yes," and you get forgiven. You feel some of the Lord's presence. You can lay hands on the sick and get results every now and then. You can preach Jesus, and your friends might get saved. That anointing for evangelism is active the first day after you have been saved. You can read the Word and get revelation. You'll feel a little bit of God's presence, which is an introductory anointing for intimacy. But never should we limit our vision to that which is given freely and is automatic. To enter into the greater realms takes a fierce determination. You enter by weakness, meaning not sinfulness but a lifestyle of fasting, prayer, serving, and bearing up under persecution. (See 2 Corinthians 11–12.)

> THERE IS A DIFFERENCE BETWEEN THE INTRODUCTORY GRACE AND ANOINTING OF GOD THAT COME TO US AT SALVATION AND THE GREATER REALMS THAT GOD GIVES THOSE WHO TAKE THE KINGDOM BY FORCE, WHO PRESS IN TO HIS HEART WITH A VISION FOR THE FULLNESS OF GOD'S POWER.

Weakness? Yes. Think of it this way. When you invest your time and energy in prayer, you are forfeiting hours and energy you could be using to build a ministry or business or lifestyle in some other way. Fasting too is about weakness. You are giving away your physical strength. Giving your money is embracing weakness by giving away your time and energy. Persecution is the same thing. Instead of getting your own vengeance, you silently bear under it, rejoicing in the Lord. Those are the four main ways in which weakness is described in 2 Corinthians 11–12 and throughout the Word of God.

The problem is that when we begin to walk down the path of weakness, the power does not break out immediately. The Lord tests our faith with a time delay. After a while we want to draw back, and that's when the Lord would say, "So you think I'm lying about this being the way to power? You think that the way to power is to skip that step and do it on your own?" You see, man's way is to rush straight into doing the works of the kingdom, bypassing the step of weakness. The message of weakness is offensive in the church. Most ministries end up believing the lie that there is more power by spending your time doing the works of the kingdom instead of taking some of that time and pouring it into the presence of God. They measure in the here and now. But in the big picture of church history, when people have persistently fasted and prayed and given their money and borne the stigma of the anointing, God has always proved true by releasing power in a greater dimension. It may take years, but it happens, without exception.

Cornelius, an unsaved Gentile, didn't go to the synagogue, had no born-again experience, no anointing, and no worship tapes, but he spent his entire life in fasting and prayer and giving gifts. Suddenly an angel came in Acts 10 and said, "You are the man to open up the Word of God to the Gentile nations." Cornelius must have thought, *I didn't think anybody was listening to me up there anymore.* It was the shock of his life.

Anna spent sixty years praying at the temple before getting a glimpse of the promise (Luke 2:37). When Jesus told the disciples in John 4 that they were entering into the labors of others, He undoubtedly had Anna in mind.

Beloved, we measure it all wrong when we measure in months or even years. Some have labored lifetimes. We must set our sights on the long view, persevering through the ups and downs of the moment. We must also embrace the full strategy of entering into God's power through weakness, and that includes the added dimension of a radical lifestyle of corporate prayer with fasting (Joel 2:12–17). That's the third facet of the apostolic faith.

Not only must we contend for power, but also we must live holy and radically abandoned to Jesus, and I believe He's calling people to do this through a lifestyle of fasting.

A Lifestyle of Fasting

Regardless of what you might think, fasting is exhilarating. It enlarges our hearts by helping us encounter the beauty of our Bridegroom. Jesus promoted fasting and introduced a new paradigm of fasting in Matthew 9, which was very different from what was known in the Old Testament.

> Then John's disciples came and asked him, "How is it that we and the Pharisees fast, but your disciples do not fast?" Jesus answered, "How can the guests of the bridegroom mourn while he is with them? The time will come when the bridegroom will be taken from them; then they will fast."
>
> —Matthew 9:14–15, NIV

Through fasting Jesus brings us into partnership with Him and opens our heart in a way that no other dimension in the grace of God can. Three things happen:

1. We receive greater measure of revelation and power.
2. We receive it faster.
3. The impact of this revelation goes deeper in us.

God uses fasting and the Word as a Holy Spirit catalyst to speed up the process and enlarge the measure and the depth of which we receive the beauty of the Lord. This yields great benefits. Jesus said:

> But when you fast, put oil on your head and wash your face, so that it will not be obvious to men that you are fasting, but only to your Father, who is unseen; and your Father, who sees what is done in secret, will reward you.
>
> —Matthew 6:17–18, NIV

Fasting has very powerful rewards that are primarily internal, aimed at the human heart. The fast of the Old Testament was mostly for external purposes, but the Bridegroom fast touches the heart. It has a different focus. As we pursue the Lord by the grace of God through the Bridegroom fast, our physical appetites, emotional appetites, and spiritual appetites change dramatically. In a word, we gain more desire. He imparts new desires of delight to us so that fasting is not drudgery but an indescribable privilege because it brings us closer to Him and His delight for us. There is nothing the human spirit craves more than to enter into these delights, but most people don't know they exist. The lifestyle of fasting is rare, and so the benefits are rare.

WE MUST SET OUR SIGHTS ON THE LONG VIEW, PERSEVERING THROUGH THE UPS AND DOWNS OF THE MOMENT.

Not only is there the impartation of new desires, but also there is the removal or diminution of sinful desires. Beloved, when our desires line up properly, life is wonderful. When our desires are out of line, life is burdensome. You might have great wealth and all the fame on earth, but when your desires are lined up wrong, life is very hard and dull and disappointing.

Fasting, rather than increasing life's drudgery, actually releases supernatural joy. The Old Testament fast was related so often to suffering, to the affliction of our body, to the affliction of our soul. That paradigm has taken root in church history. People fast to "pay the price," but I tell you there is a pleasure in fasting—and many rewards. You can very quickly grow to love fasting. You actually lament interruptions that prevent you from continuing in it for a time. I get into the rhythm of the kind of fasting I have engaged in for the last couple of years, and when something interrupts it, I never think, *Good, I can take a break. Where's the all-you-can-eat buffet?* Just the opposite—I want to return to fasting as quickly as God will allow. You will find that the hunger to experience God begins to dominate your life. It's a strange paradox that we actually hunger to fast. I believe it is going to be a common experience to love fasting. It will take some time, but in the long run this is how the body of Christ will choose to live.

I have done plenty of fasting where I did not experience any joy. That's because I didn't have my sights set on the benefits. Without a vision of the benefits, fasting is associated with despair. Let's look at some of the main benefits of a fasted lifestyle.

Fasting tenderizes the human heart to God and increases our spiritual capacity to receive from Him.

This is a stunning reality. Over time we gain a supernatural ability to feel and experience God, specifically His love, beauty, and the glory of His plan for us. Fasting helps us build the foundation of the divine romance. This is the fast John the Baptist undertook. His fast was not for miracles but for the enlargement of his heart in God. Scripture says clearly that John did no miracles. But he fasted more than anybody I know of in Scripture, with the exception of Anna. (There are no records that Anna did any miracles, either.) But John's fasting made him great before God. Gabriel appeared to John's father and said:

> For he will be great in the sight of the Lord, and shall drink neither wine nor strong drink. He will also be filled

> with the Holy Spirit, even from his mother's womb.
>
> —LUKE 1:15

In Matthew 11:11, Jesus called him the greatest man ever born of a woman. Then in John 5:35, Jesus said of John:

> He was the burning and shining lamp, and you were willing for a time to rejoice in his light.

It is possible and quite common for people to contend strongly for biblical orthodoxy or even power demonstrations, and yet have spiritually dull hearts toward Jesus. That is because they don't practice a lifestyle of fasting. They may go a lifetime working hard for sound doctrine without cultivating a spirit of tenderness in this way. In Jesus' day, the very people who insisted on biblical orthodoxy sought to kill Jesus and John the Baptist. Likewise, many Christians throughout history have studied the church fathers, memorized the lessons of history, and argued theological points without having demonstrations of power backed up by radical apostolic lifestyles.

> FASTING, RATHER THAN INCREASING LIFE'S DRUDGERY, ACTUALLY RELEASES SUPERNATURAL JOY.

If you want to be great before the Lord and have a heart tenderized toward Him, try fasting. You will understand what this reward is about.

Fasting illuminates the mind with the spirit of revelation and sharpens our understanding of the Word.

Acts 2:17 mentions a dimension of dreams and visions that I would put into this category, too. Your revelation of the things of God will increase when you fast. Since I began fasting, I have had a significant increase of spiritual dreams about Jesus related to the

Bridegroom. I have had more dreams about the Word of God, where the Lord is speaking to me about the Word, awakening my heart to specific parts that relate to my ministry. I'll tell you, there is nothing better than when Jesus preaches Jesus. That's what happened on the Emmaus road in Luke 24. Jesus appeared to the disciples and preached who He was and is. When He left, they said, "Did not our heart burn within us while He talked with us on the road?" (v. 32).

Scripture says Jesus opened their understanding, and that is what the Bridegroom fast does. It opens your understanding, either through direct study of the Word when you are awake or when the Lord begins to visit you in dreams and visions.

God opens the realm of secrets to those who draw near to Him. In John 13:25–26, John laid his head on the Lord's breast, and the Lord spoke to him about Judas, which was the first secret or scandal to hit the apostolic company. The psalmist wrote in the Book of Psalms:

> The secret of the LORD is with those who fear Him, and He will show them His covenant.
>
> —PSALM 25:14

A billion dollars cannot buy you the secrets of God. You cannot buy or manipulate your way into those regions of God's heart, but I tell you that prayer and fasting escort us there. Paul wrote:

> But God has revealed them to us through His Spirit. For the Spirit searches all things, yes, the deep things of God.
>
> —1 CORINTHIANS 2:10

Jesus said in John 16:15, "All things that the Father has are Mine. Therefore I said that He will take of Mine and declare it to you."

I want to peer into those secret things that are found by laying our head upon the breast of Jesus. There, God will give us details of how to interpret His End-Time activity, how to interpret His plans related to the Bridegroom, what to do with our time and energy, and how to work with Him in the last days.

Fasting enlarges our emotions, particularly righteousness.

Hebrews 1:8 says:

> But to the Son He says: "Your throne, O God, is forever and ever; a scepter of righteousness is the scepter of Your kingdom."

Jesus loves righteousness and hates iniquity. He has many emotions, and I want to move beyond the feelings of being loved and desired and enter into His other feelings of love for righteous and hatred of iniquity. As we fast, our emotional chemistry changes radically, not just in the realm of feeling His love, though that is the number one point, but also in having zeal for God's purpose and God's ways. We discover more of His emotions, which we didn't know He had.

Imagine living a life where your primary energies are gathered together into one intense focus, birthed by the Holy Spirit. That's what fasting does. It centers you on God's emotions. I am not saying that we get to forget the secondary issues of life—mowing the lawn, buying groceries, taking the car to be fixed. But through fasting God grants us divine perspective on life. Little things more consistently appear little, and big things more consistently appear big. Big things like eternity, the End-Time harvest, the great judgments, the shaking of Planet Earth—those are big things. But they appear little to most believers. Little things like daily annoyances, or even big-time betrayals in relationships or money, look big. In reality, those things are little.

Fasting tightens up our perspective. The big picture

becomes effortlessly more clear. We don't get bogged down in the little picture. There is a transcending in our understanding. We do not get lost in the pettiness that comes so naturally to every one of us. Fasting doesn't always remove problems; rather, problems come into divine perspective. We live more as Holy Spirit honeymooners with Jesus, preoccupied with love more than problems.

That's an exciting way to live. It's like being involved in the most exciting story plot this side of heaven. In the realm of God's emotions, that story unfolds day by day, with surprises always around the corner. Sadly, most believers are content to live lives of spiritual boredom. You can be anointed in ministry and still be absolutely bored out of your mind, not sharing God's strong spectrum of emotions. I know of several godly men who have large ministries with miracle power, and they have said to me with their own lips, "I am spiritually bored." Most believers are like that, going through the motions.

GOD OPENS THE REALM OF SECRETS TO THOSE WHO DRAW NEAR TO HIM.

I don't want to be anything less than gripped by God, and so I live a fasted lifestyle to open the realm of exploration into the unimaginable complexity and wonder of God's emotions.

Fasting gives you good decision-making power.

When your sense of God's emotions are enhanced, you are not easily swayed to make decisions based on the values of the world. You gain the power to refuse ungodly promotion and shrug off demotion. A profound example is found in John's Gospel when the people came to make Jesus king by force. They said, "We will obey you, and the army, the money, the legislation—everything—will be yours." But He said, "No!"

> Therefore when Jesus perceived that they were about to come and take Him by force to make Him king, He departed again to the mountain by Himself alone.
>
> —John 6:15

Jesus was unmoved because to Him, the "pay" was the same no matter what He did. He got satisfaction from His internal reality with the Father. Whether He raised the dead or took a nap, His feelings about Himself and about God didn't change. That's how we are to be. Most believers have no power to discern a promotion that is outside of the will of God. Promotion blinds them with euphoria, and they respond, "Wow! Yes, I'll take it! I mean, let me pray about it." Of course they'll say *yes* in a minute and a half. They lose ability to see that promotion out of the will of God is actually a distraction that weakens their heart with God.

One of the most profound examples of good perspective in decision making was a Catholic monk named Bernard of Clairvaux, who was born in 1090 and died in 1153. He is one of my favorite people in church history. He had just a small little sphere to start with, and then it grew so that the kings of France, Germany, and Italy, three of the most powerful men on the earth besides the pope, would not act in a significant way without Bernard's blessing. He would write them a letter and rebuke them, and they would change their military strategies and make peace with other nations. The four most powerful men in the earth followed his heart, this little Catholic monk in the valley of Clairvaux in France. At one point they pressed him to make him pope, and he said, "Why should I be pope when I have the nearness of God in my little hut?" So he refused to be bishop, refused to be pope, and said, "I will take one of my best guys, whom I have trained for years, and he can be pope in my place." He picked him, and the guy became pope.

Bernard has been a source of inspiration for me because, like me, his major life book was the Song of Solomon. He taught it for years and was committed to the Bridegroom fast. He did not use that language, but he taught on the fasted lifestyle for the sake of knowing the beauty of the Bridegroom God. And he gained a perspective on promotion. Fasting will increase your detachment from irrelevant opinions. They will seem weak, vain, and temporary. You will make better decisions, basing them on what's really important.

Fasting strengthens a deep sense of our spiritual identity as sons before a Father and a bride before the Bridegroom.

Many people flounder for years without a sense of being anchored, without a sense of their bearings in life. They have no clue who they really are. Paradoxically, that produces an excessive preoccupation with self, which is totally natural. It is supernatural not to have a preoccupation with self. Most people are totally obsessed with themselves. They learn manners and don't flaunt this obsession all the time, but they still live enslaved to what they look like to other people, and they get hurt when they are not noticed, even though they are polite and have enough dignity to hide it. I tell you, the Bridegroom fast strengthens our identity and weakens the hold of jealousy, envy, and insecurity in our lives. I know what it means to strive and manipulate to make a name for myself in ministry. I have done plenty of that in my day. Now I see a clearer way, which John pointed to when he said, "I am a voice; I do not have to be known." He didn't need men's opinions because he heard the voice of the Bridegroom. When you hear His voice, you are happy to be a voice.

> He who has the bride is the bridegroom; but the friend of the bridegroom, who stands and hears him, rejoices greatly because of the bridegroom's voice. Therefore this joy of mine is fulfilled.
>
> —John 3:29

John the Baptist had an inward tranquility of joy and gladness unrelated to having honor in the nation. The consensus of the nation at the end of his ministry was that he was dangerous and demonized.

> For John came neither eating nor drinking, and they say, "He has a demon."
>
> —Matthew 11:18

That must have been painful, but John's reality was, "I do not live by their voices; I live by another voice." When you hear the voice of a Bridegroom, it changes what you want and what you fear losing. Your list gets filled with things you cannot lose, like the anointing of the Spirit on your heart before God. No man can take that away from you. Nobody can imprison you and take your spirit of revelation. Nobody can cause you not to be great in the sight of the Lord. You find a new resolve, a budding fearlessness. You operate in the power of a romanced heart.

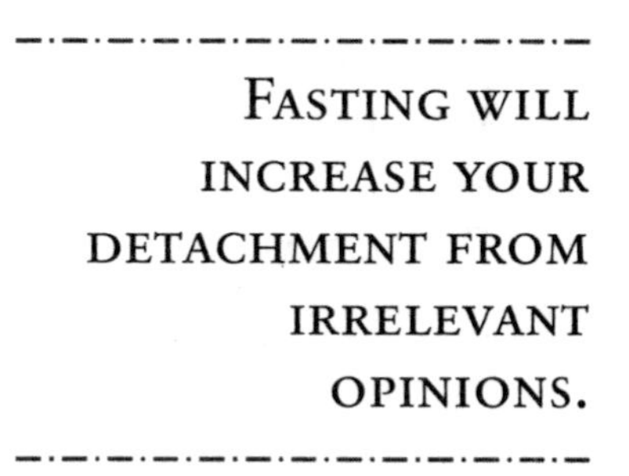

The "Violence" of Fasting

The kingdom suffers violence. "And from the days of John the Baptist until now the kingdom of heaven suffers violence, and the violent take it by force" (Matt. 11:12).

Fasting is a form of spiritual intensity, referred to here as "violence." When you read "suffers" in this verse, think of "allows" or "permits." In place of "violence," think of "spiritual intensity." This is a holy, violent love, not physical violence. From the days of the appearing of John the Baptist onward there was a new principle in the kingdom. Jesus was saying, "I am announcing something really awesome! From now on, the kingdom of God permits and rewards spiritual intensity. Spiritually intense people can take it by force of their dedication, if they want it."

John the Baptist was the picture of the ultimate measure of intensity with God. How does this relate to fasting? I believe there is no such thing as spiritual violence without fasting. Fasting is not just about food but about our motivations and habits in many areas of our life. It means paring down everything we do to serve the purpose of our Bridegroom in this generation. Fasting is not about moving God to do something. Rather, we fast because God has already moved our hearts. This fasting springs from the opposite motivation most of us are used to. If we fast to motivate God to pay attention to us, that is *legalism*. If we fast because He has paid attention to us, that is *grace*.

When men and women of God enter into spiritual violence, they will be written off as legalistic, disruptive, or morbid; eventually other believers will call them demonized, just as they labeled Jesus and John the Baptist. For a season, people who fast will be considered dangerous and legalistic within the body of Christ. I used to get hassled when the Lord would call me into new dimensions of the fasted lifestyle. Good, godly people would get uncomfortable about it until finally I put myself under a two-year gag order. When the Lord released a significant new measure of fasting in my life, I did not talk about it for two years; I didn't even talk about it with my pastoral staff. People would ask about it, and I would say, "Sorry, I'm not telling you anything." My friends at home and abroad would get so unnerved and upset and in turmoil that I would have to reassure them, "It's not about you. I am not judging anybody. I'm only thinking about God and my weak little heart growing a little bit."

When you fast in secret, it creates a whole different dynamic in your emotions because nobody can pat you on the back for it. You don't have to sort through divided emotions, and so the benefits are unlocked in your heart far more quickly. Jesus did not say to do it in secret just because it is more humble, but because it changes the emotional dynamics in you. Your motives become purified.

Anybody can fast. You can fast with no abilities, no education, and no money. All you do is . . . nothing. You dive into the Word—though it may appear dead to you—add some fasting, and lock yourself into a marathon pace of reading the Bible and telling God you love Him all day long, and I promise you in ten years you will be radically different. You will be different in only one year, though not instantly. The system doesn't work so we can go to God's bank casually and say, "I want the deep things of Your wealth, but I only have a minute." The Lord looks for hunger over time, for spiritual intensity.

IF WE FAST TO MOTIVATE GOD TO PAY ATTENTION TO US, THAT IS LEGALISM. IF WE FAST BECAUSE HE HAS PAID ATTENTION TO US, THAT IS GRACE.

In Zechariah 8:19–21, God talked about the Bridegroom fast, saying that your fast will be turned into joyful feasts before God. The communion table is an expression of the wedding table. When you fast with God, you are feasting at His table.

> Thus says the LORD of hosts: "The fast of the fourth month, the fast of the fifth, the fast of the seventh, and the fast of the tenth, shall be joy and gladness and cheerful feasts for the house of Judah. Therefore love truth and peace." Thus says the LORD of hosts: "Peoples shall yet come, inhabitants of many cities; the inhabitants of one city shall go to another, saying, 'Let us continue to go and pray before the LORD, and seek

> the LORD of hosts. I myself will go also.'"
>
> —ZECHARIAH 8:19–21

The Lord is going to raise up multitudes of people across the earth to live a fasted lifestyle before a Bridegroom God. This must happen because, beloved, everything is not all right, and all is not going to be fine if we continue on this path of insensitivity toward the purposes of God. Darkness is mounting up across the earth. This is the hour in which God's people must be endued with power and illuminating righteousness! We must roll back the epidemic in the leadership of the body of Christ.

Many pastors who once held a vision to operate in the power of God have lost their urgency for it. Once, they prayed for the sick with vibrant faith and expectancy and with prayer and fasting as a regular part of their lifestyle. Now they are content to have ministry as usual with no expectation of power. Their fire for the supernatural dimension of the faith is all but gone. Weariness has set in after plowing for all these years in the charismatic dimensions of the church. They have stopped pressing in to God's way, and they are selling out to other models of ministry and saying that God's way won't work. Yes, they may have a vision for a large church, but not an apostolic New Testament church equipped in power for the unique challenges of the end of the age.

I cannot tell you the pain I have had over dear friends who were pressing hard with me in revival for years. Many of them now won't even allow someone to mention revival or the power of God in their presence because they gave it three or four or five years and wanted God to fulfill their expectations in their time frame. It makes them angry and causes them pain. They contended for the fullness, but they had an agenda and a condition they placed on God, and now they have God on probation because He "didn't come through." I told them even back then, "Guys, we're doing this to the end." They said, "Yes, yes!" But somewhere in their spirits, they had an escape hatch.

Beloved, we do not want to give ourselves an "out"! We cannot become spiritually domesticated, seduced, and lulled to sleep by man-pleasing Western church culture. Spiritual darkness is growing at a fast pace across the earth. This is a crucial time in history. We must cry, "No! It is not OK for the church to continue in business as usual without apostolic power!" The Lord wants us to rise from our apathy and get a fresh vision for His fullness. He wants us to be like David, Peter, Paul—committed to genuine apostolic faith. We don't just want a little bit here and there. I'm talking about a day when we cast demons out of insane kids, heal paralytics by one word, empty out insane asylums—that's what I mean by deliverance. Stadiums filled, apostolic teams of young and old alike sent out to the nations of the world. Tens of thousands of churches planted, miracles beyond measure breaking forth.

I WANT TO CHALLENGE YOU TO DARE TO BELIEVE ALL THE WAY, WITH NO WAY OUT. LET'S GO FOR BROKE.

I want to challenge you to dare to believe all the way, with no way out. Let's go for broke. Let's go for the whole thing. Cut the excess out of your life. Get focused. Get ordered. Measure your life by hours, not months. Fill your spirit with revelation. Get trained. Get equipped. Get in the middle of what God is doing. Get your hands out of your pockets. Lay them on the sick, even when you feel nothing. Go for it!

The Breaker Anointing

We need men and women who have a "breaker anointing." Micah prophesied about a future day when the Messiah would lead Israel with such an anointing. In other words, He would help

Israel break out of the old way and break open new dimensions of the purpose of God.

> I will surely gather the remnant of Israel....They shall make a loud noise because of so many people. The one who breaks open will come up before them; they will break out...with the LORD at their head.
>
> —MICAH 2:12

Jesus is the ultimate expression of the breaker anointing, one who breaks open new dimensions of the Spirit for others to enter into. Today, the multitudes will only enter into the fullness of God's purpose when forerunners rise up with a breaker anointing and break us out of status quo Christianity. Forerunners break *out* in order to break *open*. They first break out of unbiblical paradigms of ministry and church life. There are many paradigms in the church today that are ungodly and not energized by the Holy Spirit. It's not easy to break out of them. Why? Because the majority of leaders and believers are bound by what those around them think. It takes a lot of emotional energy to manage all the fear, questioning, and manipulation that come when you want to please everyone. Few want to bother with breaking into new areas because they are just learning to manage the old ones.

IT'S HIGH TIME TO BREAK FREE FROM THE FEAR OF BEING CONSIDERED TOO FANATICAL.

It's high time to break free from the fear of being considered too fanatical. Beloved, we are so easily enslaved by the opinions of people. We shouldn't feel the need to apologize for our lifestyle in God. We don't have to look respectable to other Christians. Many religious paradigms we hold dear today will be shattered by the Lord Himself. We should follow Him and embrace the breaker anointing He is giving to many of us. As we break out, God will use us to break open new dimensions in the Holy Spirit to the spiritually stagnant Western church. He will make the End-Time church a dwelling place of God's power. He will release a corporate anointing where cancer, AIDS, disease, demons of pornography, drugs, and alcohol cannot survive. The Holy Spirit is raising up forerunners today who will break out and break through because they are people of one thing, contending for the power of God and the fullness of the apostolic faith.

It is not a matter of praying harder to convince God to release His power. Revival doesn't come because of more prayer meetings, more extended worship services, better music, more fasting, harder preaching, and a whole host of efforts we undertake to persuade Him to come close. As we will see in the next chapter, the opposite is true. God is not waiting to be convinced to release His power—He is waiting to convince us. He wants to give us the fullness of power for our generation, but only after He has established an intimacy with us so that we are able to handle it.

Chapter Nine

CONTENDING FOR POWER IN INTIMACY

I remember when God called me to be an intercessor in May 1979. It was one of those real-life encounters when God grabbed hold of my life and apprehended me and said, "You are an intercessor." I got up in front of my church and said, "I am an intercessor." They said, "What's that?" I said, "I don't have a clue." I truly had no idea what an intercessor was. I went to the bookstores in town and bought both books on intercession. There were hardly any—just a few standards by Andrew Murray, maybe Watchman Nee, Dick Eastman, E. M. Bounds, Leonard Ravenhill. But I tried to move ahead in it anyway, and I began daily prayer meetings, which I've held 99 percent of the days since then. I was so clueless the first time that I didn't even know what we would pray, so I wrote out by hand the apostolic prayers. I couldn't think of anything to pray. I photocopied the handwritten prayers and gave them to both guys who showed up for the first prayer meeting. That was the beginning of my education in prayer and intercession.

For years and years our church rarely saw more than twenty or thirty people in a prayer meeting. It didn't matter. I knew what God had told me, and I was grieved in my heart about the powerlessness of the church. It reminded me of one of the saddest moments in the Gospels, when a father brought his demonized son to Jesus and complained about the powerlessness of His disciples.

> A man came to Him . . . saying, "Lord, have mercy on my son, for he is an epileptic and suffers severely; for he often falls into the fire and often into the water. So I brought him to Your disciples, but they could not cure him." Then Jesus answered and said, ". . . Bring him here to Me." And Jesus rebuked the demon, and it came out of him; and the child was cured from that very hour. Then the disciples came to Jesus privately and said, "Why could we not cast him out?" So Jesus said to them, ". . . However, this kind does not go out except by prayer and fasting."
>
> —Matthew 17:14–21

This verse pains my soul to this day because it describes the common experience of the church in the Western world today. We have compassion for the downcast and demonized, but we too often lack the breakthrough power to deliver them. So I began to pray about that and many other things. I wanted to invite the power of God into my life and my church in greater measure. I didn't know I would wait years for the breakthrough of God. I didn't realize that the Lord wanted to develop a deep root system within others and within me through the process of learning to pray, and that He would do this before He began to release power in greater measure.

When I first started down this road, my idea of prayer was very different from what it is today, and I was perplexed as I began to understand God's process for bringing powerful breakthroughs. I remember my first approach to intercession. I decided I was going to convince God to move in power. That didn't last long because I soon realized that God was convincing me that He wanted to move in power. I eventually discovered that intercession was not an issue of convincing God to send revival. Through intercession, God began to convince me of what was already so clear to Him. After a while, I finally got out of the "convince God" mode. He was already convinced. I was wasting my time.

I left that season and entered a new one with a completely different approach to prayer. I began to try to earn His answer. I tried to show God through my dedication just how deserving I was. I tried to give Him a dedication so sterling, so historic, so above and beyond what had been done before that even God could not turn me down. I plunged into ultra-dedication mode, spending copious amounts of energy in prayer and service, but that approach bombed just as the first approach had. I had so many black marks on my record. I was so weak, I kept blowing it. I thought many times, *If I could just get rid of those weaknesses, then He would see how deserving I am and answer me.* But I never reached that magic place of perfection, and I realized I never would. I had gone into another cul-de-sac.

After trying to earn it and trying to convince God, I finally surrendered to Him and asked for His leading. I was perplexed and a little dismayed at what I felt He wanted me to do: go into a room by myself and repeat back to Him what He wanted me to say, much of it from the Word of God. I said, "Lord, I have so much to offer You, and yet You have me here in a room doing this odd, sort of repetitive thing. I could have won a city for You by now if You would have just let me go. Who invented running the kingdom this way?"

I was antsy to do something big and bold, to make great strides in kingdom work, but God had me tethered to this strange little habit called intercession. He had me repeating back to Him what He told me to tell Him in the Word. I thought it was the weirdest setup, and for some years it was a great mystery to me. Yet I still did it. I was not always good at it and didn't always like it, but I kept praying. I agreed to practice intercession and even to preach on it, but in secret I told the Lord I thought it was a very strange way to run the kingdom. I was actually offended by it. It didn't seem like a good use of human resources.

Contending: Developing Intimacy in the Process

Some years went by, and then God's ultimate purpose and method began to make sense to me. There was a tenderizing going on. His purpose for prayer is *intimacy*. If God causes us to cry out and then in time answers our cry, we are stunned. We marvel, we sit back in surprise, and we connect the dots of what's happening: when we speak on earth, He moves in heaven. This amazing revelation causes intimacy to increase and abound. We say from the depth of our heart, "Wow! You heard me, and You're moving. I love You! You love me! I get it!"

I EVENTUALLY DISCOVERED THAT INTERCESSION WAS NOT AN ISSUE OF CONVINCING GOD TO SEND REVIVAL.

When we realize that divine action is taken when we cry out, it awakens us to love. It attaches our heart strongly to His. The Lord may give us a long history of crying out to Him, but then in time He gives an answer to every single prayer that we pray. There is not a wasted prayer. He doesn't just wow us by letting us see the breakthrough and the increase. He causes the place of prayer to become *the place of encounter* with Him. We grow in an open spirit toward the throne simply by the repetition and washing of His Word over our hearts.

A key ingredient in this is perseverance. When God gives a vision, He gives a promise. He begins to release it into manifestation, but perhaps not on our time schedule—and certainly not on the schedule I originally wanted for myself. Though we experience rest in the inner man, we fight and struggle in our outer man to stick with the process of learning to cultivate intimacy through prayer and a lifestyle of fasting. God gives many promises in His Word about persevering in the heat of the battle. He speaks of answering the call and sticking with it through boredom, rotten times, and the bad advice of friends. Hebrews 6:12 says that we inherit the promises through faith and perseverance. First, we inherit them by faith, and then we realize them by refusing to let them go through hardship and the passing of time.

Isaiah sheds light on this aspect of our walk with God in Isaiah 30:18.

> Therefore the LORD will wait, that He may be gracious to you.... Blessed are all those who wait for Him.

The Lord longs to be gracious to us, but He won't when it threatens to alienate us from Him. He longs to show ever so much more grace than we ask Him for, but He will not break through in a way that undermines bridal intimacy with His church. He wants to do amazing things on earth, but He wants to do it in partnership with us. In our natural mind-set, we imagine that God will bring revival in a specific city for a specific season simply because He desires it. We think He will be gracious to us and release the breakthrough simply because He longs to be gracious. We want it sooner rather than later. We think we're ready for anything.

God does want to do this, but He will do it through bridal partnership. That means we have a part to play. What is the delay we so often experience? The Lord is waiting for our cry of agreement. We think we are convincing Him, but God is saying in effect, "I am convincing you about My longing, and I want you to reciprocate that longing. I will wait until I hear the sound of the wholehearted cry of My people before I give you what you're praying for." He does this to establish intimate partnership with His bride. If He releases His grace in fullness apart from intimate relationship, the people of God will get so captured by the release of grace, so thrilled by the breaking in of the supernatural, that they will get distracted along the way and forsake relationship.

It was the Lord's idea to be gracious to us, not our own. He longs to be gracious far more than we long for Him to be. But that grace must establish His relationship with us, not undermine it. Therefore He will not release it in fullness until He hears the great cry of His people, signifying our readiness. Though He will release a certain administration of grace no matter what, He's looking forward to giving more than that introductory dimension of the kingdom of God. History has proven that when the Lord releases a breakthrough before the church is ready to do its part in the relationship, the very release pulls people quickly off track. All the converts, the miracles, the numbers, the promises, the power, the supernatural activity—even a small increase of anointing on the Word—cause

HE CAUSES THE PLACE OF PRAYER TO BECOME THE PLACE OF ENCOUNTER WITH HIM.

us to lose our way if it's independent of our sustained cry as a corporate body. It has happened many times, often just a few years after revival begins. People get distracted by other things, and over time their hearts become like a field that has been burned. It's hard to grow anything there again.

The Lord avoids this trap of the enemy by holding back His breakthrough and anointing and letting the cry of our hearts arise. He is already convinced of what He wants to do. But He convinces us of what is in His heart as we cry out to Him day after day. We do not earn anything by crying out. We cannot sing or shout and earn power. Rather, the Lord's plan is that when we lift our voices to Him, our hearts become receptive and connected to Him. When that happens, we enter a realm where God's blessing and grace actually establish and enhance intimacy with God instead of diminishing it. Revival now strengthens the partnership. The process of prayer has surprised, tenderized, and drawn into intimacy with Him. That "tenderization" and intimacy protect us under the weight of revival when the Lord releases it.

So the Lord cultivates intimacy in our relationship with Him by delaying His answer until we cry out. Sometimes He even delays the answer for years. Yet when it finally happens, we feel joy just as a mother experiences joy after the pain of childbirth. The presence of the child, this wonderful gift, causes the memory of the pain to fade away (John 16:21). Whether the answer comes in a day, a month, or ten years from when we begin, our hearts are stunned when God breaks in. Yet this brilliant strategy of God is about more than surprise. It's about the transformation that happens to us in the process of learning to pray.

Our prayer meetings will not force God to answer us. We cannot in any way do anything to deserve supernatural power. The economy of heaven never works that way. We are in a time of preparation. God is preparing a root system and a foundation for what He will give us in His grace. The longer the time of delay, the greater the joy when the answer comes. More than that, the change that happens to us in the process will protect us when the answer comes.

> THE LORD CULTIVATES INTIMACY IN OUR RELATIONSHIP WITH HIM BY DELAYING HIS ANSWER UNTIL WE CRY OUT.

God desires more than our endurance and patience in prayer. He wants us to open our mind and spirits to Him in all the seasons of life. It can be difficult at times, but the Lord desires people of one thing, contending for the fullness of God in every season. David was such a man, and we will draw invaluable lessons from his life as we continue to study this third major aspect of becoming men and women after God's own heart.

Chapter Ten

DAVID: CONTENDING FOR GOD'S FULLNESS

David was a lot like many Christians today. He didn't just want to be a man of obedience and intimacy. He wanted to see the power of God released in his nation and in his personal life. This pursuit pleases God. The Bible says, "The eyes of the LORD run to and fro throughout the whole earth, to show Himself strong on behalf of those whose heart is loyal to Him" (2 Chron. 16:9). The Lord at this very moment is searching for men and women whose hearts can be fully His. He is looking for that capital Y-E-S in people's spirits.

Some mistakenly believe that they must be without weakness in order to contend for and receive God's power. They imagine some perfect, totally righteous person being endued with the power of the Holy Spirit, but they never picture themselves doing great works of power for God. They know their own faults too well. The good news from David's life, which we touched on earlier, is that not only does God allow us to draw close to Him in intimacy in spite of our failings, but He also encourages us to pursue His power even when we are weak. David's life is a witness that weakness does not disqualify us from experiencing God's power.

> Incline your ear, and come to Me.... I will make an everlasting covenant with you—the sure mercies of David. Indeed I have given him as a witness to the people.
>
> —Isaiah 55:3–4

Isaiah tells us that God raised up David as a testimony that God's mercies are for those who cry out for them. In this passage, the Lord had made a covenant with the people that He would show them the same mercies He showed David. When we press in to God even in our weakness, God promises to relate to us in the same way that He related to David. This means that even in our weakness we can go hard after God and expect a breakthrough. We don't have to abandon our spiritual pursuit when we stumble. With confidence we can press in to the power of God. Yes, it's hard sometimes. We grow weary and faint in our pursuit of Jesus. But we are never told to stop pursuing His power.

I have often drawn strength from the story of Gideon's army in pursuit of their enemies, the Midianite army. They grew weary in the pursuit. Scripture says, "Gideon came to Jordan, and passed over, he, and the three hundred men that were with him, faint, yet pursuing them" (Judg. 8:4, KJV). When we get weary and faint in our spiritual pursuit, we must continue on because we will have a breakthrough in God's time!

David's Longing for a Dwelling Place for God

To be people after God's own heart, we must do as David did and vow to pursue God's power until it is established on the earth.

> LORD, remember David and all his afflictions; how he swore to the LORD, and vowed to the Mighty One of Jacob: "Surely I will not go into the chamber of my house, or go up to the comfort of my bed; I will not give sleep to my eyes or slumber to my eyelids, *until* I find a place for the LORD, a dwelling place for the Mighty One of Jacob."
>
> —PSALM 132:1–5, EMPHASIS ADDED

A dwelling place for God speaks of the place where God's power is openly manifest to bring freedom and victory to multitudes. A habitation speaks of longevity, more than the short visitations of revival our generation has often experienced. It was not enough for David to seek the Lord privately and experience the pleasures of gazing on His beauty. He wanted a demonstration of God's power in Israel for all the nations to see so they would fear the Lord. So intensely did this zeal burn within him that he swore to the Mighty One that he would not pursue his own personal comfort until there was a habitation of the power of God in Israel.

DAVID'S LIFE IS A WITNESS THAT WEAKNESS DOES NOT DISQUALIFY US FROM EXPERIENCING GOD'S POWER.

Does this describe you? Will you do whatever it takes to see a spiritual breakthrough in your city that results in a long-term habitation of God? David was willing to make sacrifices to see that habitation established. You and I should also yearn to see the habitation of God—a place where God lives and manifests His glory and power over the long term, not just for short seasons of revival.

God wants to do it! He wants to release His power and authority to us as He did to David. Isaiah prophesied to Eliakim:

> The key of the house of David I will lay on his shoulder; so shall he open, and no one shall shut; and he shall shut, and no one shall open.
>
> —Isaiah 22:22

Jesus quoted this prophecy and applied it to His church. Jesus has the authority of David, and He will release it to His servants in the church, as we see in Revelation:

> ...He [Jesus] who has the key of David, He who opens and no one shuts, and shuts and no one opens...I have set before you an open door, and no one can shut it.
>
> —Revelation 3:7–8

This is a promise for people after God's own heart. When we seek Him and His power in obedience and intimacy, Jesus releases the authority to open and shut doors in the Spirit. This is how He interacts with you and me. Jesus prophesied that His disciples would experience an open heaven, speaking of opening a doorway of blessing in the Spirit. Jesus said, "Most assuredly, I say to you, hereafter you shall see heaven open, and the angels of God ascending and descending upon the Son of Man" (John 1:51). We are invited to live under that open heaven!

> **God wants to do it! He wants to release His power and authority to us as He did to David.**

When God finds a corporate people wholeheartedly pursuing Him with the heart of David, He will open and shut doors in the spirit and in the natural. Doors of darkness will be shut in the spirit, and evil things in the natural will dry up. Positive doors of light and righteousness will be opened in the spirit, and righteous things in the natural will flourish. We are to be a people of power, opening and shutting doors according to the will and power of the Lord.

Bearing the Reproach

I mentioned before, and I want to discuss it more fully here, that there is an inevitable reproach and stigma that come with pursuing the fullness of God. People get easily troubled by the pathway into the power of God. It involves prayer with fasting. It is a journey that's invasive, unbiased, not connected to political movements or cultural shifts. It doesn't fit into Western society in a comfortable way, but instead it presses in to the private places and makes unrelenting demands on your soul. David said, "Because for Your sake I have borne reproach; shame has covered my face. I have become a stranger to my brothers, and an alien to my mother's children; because zeal for Your house has eaten me up" (Ps. 69:7–9). David's own family members mocked him because of his passionate pursuit of God, which included prayer with fasting. They shook their heads and even wrote him off. This estrangement was because of his zeal for the house of God. His heart was alive with the vision to see the house of God established. He could not live the way he used to live until there was a release of the manifest power and glory of God in the land (Ps. 132:1–5).

> Because zeal for Your house has eaten me up, and the reproaches of those who reproach You have fallen on me. When I wept and chastened my soul with fasting, that became my reproach. I also made sackcloth my garment; I became a byword to them. Those who sit in the gate speak against me, and I am the song of the drunkards.
>
> —Psalm 69:9–12

People in Israel, the very redeemed people of God, were upset with David because of his love for God. They looked for any mistake he might make so they could discredit his zeal. Why? Because they felt convicted by his lifestyle. They wanted to find fault with him so they would be off the hook. They probably said things like, "David, are you trying to tell me I'm supposed to live like you're living?" David would respond, "No, I am not even talking to you. I need more of God." Without his saying a word, they felt judged as carnal and ungodly.

The definition of a fanatic is someone who loves Jesus more than you do. Fiery lifestyles disrupt religious people. Religious systems and people resist abandonment because it threatens their stability and power. There are few radical believers in the Western church today, and yet people who drink from the well of Western values are greatly offended by these passionate, sold-out believers. It unnerves them. They feel judged by the lifestyle. They don't like the "in-your-face" prophetic statement that an abandoned lifestyle makes. Like David's family, they want to write you off so they can soothe their consciences and settle down into business as usual without disruptions.

This conflict is only going to increase in the years to come. Fearless, wholehearted believers will be in the *majority* before the Lord returns. But on the way there, in the years that lie ahead, there will be great unsettledness in the body of Christ as radical fasting-and-praying believers upset the status quo. These people are no better than anyone else; they don't form a new spiritual elite. (They will be hungrier, but not better!) But they will cause all kinds of turbulence for a few decades as they go after their goal with great zeal even in their weakness. Others will feel judged. People will transfer their anger and bitterness toward God to these believers.

When David arose with consuming zeal, people who were mad at God took it out on David. This got worse when David prayed and fasted. "When I wept and chastened my soul with fasting, that became my reproach" (v. 10). The leaders and elders spoke against him, and even the drunkards mocked him and sang songs about him (v. 12).

When prayer and fasting are added to zeal for God's house, those around you will go from irritation to outright anger. They will say things like, "Oh, so now you're the one who is really close to God, right?" This reaction from family and friends may shock you the way it shocked David.

John the Baptist experienced the same reproach. People said even worse things about him than they did about David. Jesus described him as one who "came neither eating nor drinking." In other words, He came in the grace of fasting, and the people said, "He has a demon" (Matt. 11:18). When John's ministry was originally launched, for a short season the nation of Israel rejoiced in it (John 5:35). Yet their enthusiasm faded and died like a flower in the heat of the sun. Soon they said he was demonized and dangerous to the community. Yet Jesus called John the greatest man ever born of a woman (Matt. 11:11).

> IT IS IMPORTANT TO STAY STEADY WITH HUMILITY AS YOU CONTEND FOR APOSTOLIC FAITH AND A BREAKTHROUGH OF THE HOLY SPIRIT IN YOUR CITY AND YOUR LIFE.

So be warned: contending for the power of God with intimacy is disruptive. You will be confronted and criticized for your lifestyle. Beloved, the people of God in our culture and in this time of history will not all applaud your consuming zeal for Jesus. A fiery life provokes fire in return—even friendly fire from family and acquaintances. They will come up with theological, emotional, and relational arguments to write you off. You will feel the stigma placed on you, and you will bear the reproach that David and John the Baptist bore. A lifestyle of one thing and contending for God's power is like drawing a line in the sand. It says God has higher levels than we live in now. It is a statement that demands a response. Be prepared, so that when it comes, you don't quit. It is important to stay steady with humility as you contend for apostolic faith and a breakthrough of the Holy Spirit in your city and your life.

On the other hand, some people welcome this revelation. When a stagnant and spiritually dull person touches passion in the life of another, it awakens or hardens him or her. Paul spoke of this principle in 2 Corinthians 2:16 as being life to life, or death to death. An unbeliever can touch a man or a woman with this kind of passion, be awakened out of spiritual slumber, and become a fiery new convert. He or she moves from death to life. A lethargic pastor can touch the passion in a young person and be awakened, moving from life to life. Someone who has been in the body of Christ for forty years might touch this zeal in someone else's heart and experience godly jealousy to move forward in God. It's an amazing thing. Vibrant lives that burn with righteousness are never neutral. They affect lives around them, either sparking the same holy flame or inspiring anger and rebuke.

But that's the battle we are called to. As we become people of one thing, it is not enough to be obedient and discover God's emotions. We must also contend for a manifest dwelling of God in the earth. His power is worth it, and He will release it in due time as we persevere in intimacy through the inevitable reproach.

The life of David gives us a beautiful road map for becoming people after God's heart. That road map unfolds as we see the five prophetic seasons of David's life—and the five prophetic seasons of our own journey to maturity.

Chapter Eleven

THE FIVE PROPHETIC SEASONS OF DAVID'S LIFE

How did David become the great warrior king and lover of God we know him as today? Was he born that way? No. He had the raw material for greatness, as we all do, but David had to go through seasons of preparation, just as we all go through seasons in becoming men and women after God's own heart. We are privileged through Scripture to know more about David's life than about any other biblical person besides Jesus. We know he was told he would be king at about age seventeen. We know that God then took him through a twenty-year prophetic journey of preparation marked by five different seasons that would equip him for his calling. These five seasons speak to us as we seek to become men and women after God's heart. They mark the path we must follow to achieve that vision, which includes the full measure of power and intimacy with God we seek.

David's life is a prophetic picture of how God brings us into the fullness of our calling by establishing our identity in the Lord.

God brings us through specific stages of preparation so we can inherit all He has promised us. Unfortunately for us, humans don't learn well in good circumstances, so the Lord often trains us in the midst of problems. In those seasons, we put down roots in Him as our sole source of validation.

Each season in David's life had a specific city and a specific lesson associated with it. The cities are:

1. Bethlehem
2. Gibeah
3. Adullam
4. Hebron
5. Zion

Let's apply the lessons we encounter in each of these to our own journeys as we seek to become people with hearts after God's.

Bethlehem: Faithfulness in Small Things

Like Jesus many years later, David was born in Bethlehem, the youngest of eight sons of Jesse and the lowest in rank and privilege in the family structure. In his early years, he became a shepherd. As we have seen, keeping the sheep in that society was not a distinguished occupation. If the family could afford it, they delegated this dirty task to the servants. But in Jesse's family, the job fell to David. So, like other shepherds, he stood around all day on the hard rocks, alone under the hot sun with the sheep as his only companions. We like to imagine David sitting in the shade on the hillside with lush, green grass and sheep gathered around him like fluffy cotton balls. We think of him as a modern farm boy, a Huck Finn lying on his back admiring the sky with a stalk of hay between his teeth. But that's not how the story went. David lived for several years in what amounted to solitary confinement in a desert environment. His flock was small, so he was the only one needed to do the tiresome work (1 Sam. 17:28). He was very much alone in harsh terrain.

You have to wonder what God saw in David that He didn't see in his brothers, who are little known except as scoffers. The key is in these Bethlehem years. David was too young to have done anything extraordinary. He hadn't cast out demons, healed the sick, or preached anointed sermons. His great exploits all lay in the future. The only portrayal we find of him during this time is of him keeping the sheep (1 Sam. 16:11). We might think of him as a gas station attendant or a janitor. His life was filled with menial tasks nobody wanted to do, yet he did them with a spirit of devotion toward the Lord. That was David's first victory. He had a heart that sought God when seeking God seemed the least obvious thing to do. In the midst of the long and lonely days, David was having dynamic interaction with God in his heart. He had a *yes* in his spirit, even in his routine, boring job.

DAVID'S LIFE IS A PROPHETIC PICTURE OF HOW GOD BRINGS US INTO THE FULLNESS OF OUR CALLING BY ESTABLISHING OUR IDENTITY IN THE LORD.

When no one was looking, he was faithful with little things and resolute in his responsibilities. He risked his life to kill a lion and a bear to protect his father's sheep. Later, when he was talking to Saul about Goliath, Saul asked him, "Why do you think you can defeat Goliath?" David said, in essence, "Well, the Lord's already been with me. My dad told me to take care of the sheep, so when a lion and bear came after the sheep, I took a sword and killed them." (See 1 Samuel 17:35.) It reminds me of what Proverbs 20:6 says: "Most men will proclaim each his own goodness, but who can find a faithful man?" Many proclaim they are faithful and good, but who can find a faithful man when no one is looking? David was such a man, and you and I are to be such people, even in the desert times.

There in Bethlehem, David received God's call on his life. God's primary earthly goal for David was to make him a worshiping warrior king, being loved by God and being a lover of God. We read that:

> Now the LORD said to Samuel, "How long will you mourn for Saul, seeing I have rejected him from reigning over Israel? Fill your horn with oil, and go; I am sending you to Jesse the Bethlehemite. For I have provided Myself a king among his sons."
>
> —1 SAMUEL 16:1

We too will receive the first confirmation of our calling in our own "Bethlehem." God's sequence of events works like this: when we are faithful in small beginnings, the Lord begins to release some of His promises concerning our destiny. It's like the first waters of spring running down a formerly dry creek bed. For David, that day came without warning. He had no clue, as far as we know, that he was destined to sit on the throne. He was one of hundreds of ordinary young men living in Israel. We can only imagine he didn't have a huge vision for his career. But one day, Samuel, the most famous person in Israel, came to Jesse's home for dinner, surely one of the greatest occasions in that household's history up to that point. Jesse invited seven sons but did not invite David. He was left out in the pasture with the sheep.

Imagine being shunned by your own father on such a rare and sacred occasion. Even Jesse didn't see what God saw in David's heart. But Samuel called for the youngest boy and prophesied that amazing days were ahead for David. Those first waters of spring began to flow. David was ushered into a new era of knowing what was ahead of him. I can picture the utter astonishment of his father and brothers as the oil flowed down his face and neck—their little shepherd, a king?

Many people in the church have had similar experiences. They are residing in their personal Bethlehem when one day they run smack into the call of God on their lives. Someone prophesies about their future, and they taste those first waters of spring. Suddenly, they understand that they have a place in God's plan that goes beyond what they had considered. They get chills of joy, and their mind does overtime thinking of the possibilities. They want to stay up all night planning their future.

That's natural, and the Lord rejoices with us in the excitement of that moment, but we must keep in mind that this is only the very beginning of the journey. David received the prophecy from Samuel when he was about seventeen years old. But he didn't become king of Israel until he was thirty-seven! Twenty years of monumental ups and downs lay between him and the earthly prize of reaching Zion, his place of destiny. Think of that. David had no idea the promise would take twenty years to come to pass.

> GOD'S SEQUENCE OF EVENTS WORKS LIKE THIS: WHEN WE ARE FAITHFUL IN SMALL BEGINNINGS, THE LORD BEGINS TO RELEASE SOME OF HIS PROMISES CONCERNING OUR DESTINY.

You too may have received a first prophecy or insight into what you will accomplish for God. The automatic response is to say, "Let's get to it, Lord! Bring it on." You want to speed all the way to the finish line without stopping. But you must thoroughly absorb the lessons of Bethlehem. The small days are for a reason.

Most people might have stewed in anger during those years,

wanting to leave the grubby tasks and get on to the big stuff. But David somehow used the time to grow in intimacy with God. Though he had no recognition from his family, he knew he had great value from his relationship with God. He fulfilled his demeaning responsibilities with integrity of heart and skillfulness of hands (Ps. 78:70–72). He became a genuine worshiper of God.

In our own lives, the small days will make us faithful in small things so we can be trusted later with big things. The Lord said through Zechariah, "Who despises the day of small things?" (Zech. 4:10, NIV). And Jesus said, "And if you have not been faithful in what is another man's, who will give you what is your own?" (Luke 16:12). We have to be faithful in serving others before God gives us our own. And we must be faithful in natural things to be entrusted with heavenly things. Nobody starts with a large stadium ministry or a large business or a worldwide healing center. We start by setting patterns of righteous behavior in small matters: paying our bills, being honest in our relationships, following through with commitments, taking blame when necessary, managing another person's money or ministry well. Jesus gave us a foundational kingdom principle that only when we are faithful over few things will He make us ruler over many things (Matt. 25:21). This promise has its fulfillment in this age and in the age to come, but the promise always starts with few things. That is what Bethlehem represents.

This is also the place where we learn to find our satisfaction not in the prophecy or promise but in God. He must be the sole source of our identity. Every ounce of David's identity, value, and success was established in his being loved by God and being a lover of God—nothing more, nothing less. That rootedness would help him be a successful king many years later.

You can tell when a person is finding his or her identity in the task or promise because he tries to force the fulfillment of the promises on his life. He strives to advance, strives to gain favor with powerful people. He spreads tension to people around him with a competitive, impatient spirit. You can tell something's not right, because you know the person is called of God, but there's a division in his spirit. It doesn't make sense outwardly, but inwardly he is struggling mightily to define his identity.

This has probably happened to you at one time or another. The only remedy is to return to your roots and find your identity in God alone. Only in that revelation will you learn to live in peace, with the absence of striving. You find great joy in small tasks, as David did being a shepherd long after Samuel's visit was a mere memory. Bethlehem is the place to discover that your success comes not from what you do, but from who you are in God.

David latched on to this truth at an amazingly young age. He already felt successful because of his relationship with God. He was not in a frenzied panic to make sure people recognized his calling, like many in the church today. He derived his sense of greatness by being loved and being a lover of God. That should be our model. We all want to feel important, but when we truly embrace the deep revelation of God's heart for us, the struggle to feel important is settled. We don't seek importance in our job, other people, our marriage or children, or in our ministry or service to the church. We know our great value is hidden in Him.

WE HAVE TO BE FAITHFUL IN SERVING OTHERS BEFORE GOD GIVES US OUR OWN. AND WE MUST BE FAITHFUL IN NATURAL THINGS TO BE ENTRUSTED WITH HEAVENLY THINGS.

Each of us starts in Bethlehem, finding our identity in God and becoming faithful in small things. It would be much nicer, from a carnal perspective, to skip Bethlehem and go right to Zion.

But the journey to our highest destiny starts with little responsibilities. It may mean being neglected, pushed aside, and ignored. But this significant season lays the foundation for success later on. It's an essential, inescapable part of the journey from which nobody is exempt, not even the Messiah. Both David and Jesus had their small beginnings in Bethlehem, yet both were destined to rule with God's authority. If the eternal King started in Bethlehem, so will anyone who follows Him.

Gibeah: The Test of Early Promotion

> Therefore Saul sent messengers to Jesse, and said, "Send me your son David, who is with the sheep."... So David came to Saul and stood before him. And he loved him greatly, and he became his armorbearer. Then Saul sent to Jesse, saying, "Please let David stand before me, for he has found favor in my sight."
>
> —1 Samuel 16:19–22

After Samuel anointed David, the Spirit of the Lord departed from Saul, and a distressing spirit troubled him. As a cure for his ugly mood, Saul's servants recommended David to play music to comfort him. They referred to David as "skillful in playing... prudent in speech, and a handsome person; and the Lord is with him" (1 Sam. 16:18). So David moved to the city of Gibeah, the capital of Saul's government (1 Sam. 15:34; 18:2). He lived there from approximately the time he was seventeen to when he was twenty-three. Saul was greatly pleased with him, and David found favor in Saul's eyes. David also found favor with the entire nation of Israel, which had been in full-scale military crisis because of Goliath the Philistine. David was used by God to pull the nation out of a disaster. He became a national hero and brought the nation into a significant victory.

The Philistines stood on a mountain on one side, and Israel stood on a mountain on the other side, with a valley between them.

> And a champion went out from the camp of the Philistines, named Goliath.... Then he stood and cried out to the armies of Israel, and said to them, "...Choose a man for yourselves, and let him come down to me. If he is able to fight with me and kill me, then we will be your servants. But if I prevail against him and kill him, then you shall be our servants and serve us." ...When Saul and all Israel heard these words of the Philistine, they were dismayed and greatly afraid....
>
> Then David said to Saul, "Let no man's heart fail because of him; your servant will go and fight with this Philistine."
>
> And Saul said to David, "You are not able to go against this Philistine to fight with him; for you are a youth, and he a man of war from his youth."
>
> ...Then David said to the Philistine, "You come to me with a sword, with a spear, and with a javelin. But I come to you in the name of the LORD of hosts.... This day the LORD will deliver you into my hand...that all the earth may know that there is a God in Israel...."
>
> ...So David prevailed over the Philistine with a sling and a stone, and struck the Philistine and killed him....Now the men of Israel and Judah arose and shouted, and pursued the Philistines.
>
> —1 SAMUEL 17:3–52

In this second season of life, David had his first taste of earthly success, and it was significant. In our day, his invitation to work at the king's side as his personal armorbearer would be like the president of the United States asking a teenager to work as an aide in the White House. Such a person would be a celebrity wunderkind. So the whole nation of Israel knew about David. He went from tending sheep to serving the king in one day. The nation raved about him in popular songs of the day. God snatched him out of the hills of Bethlehem, significantly increased his salary, and gave him favor before man.

What David probably didn't know is that in all this early success, God was testing the character of his love and servanthood. Would he continue to draw on his spiritual identity in God, or would he begin to find value and importance from his new position of honor? This was the test of promotion God set before David in Gibeah.

Blessing tests us differently than adversity. Before blessing comes, we imagine we will be so faithful to handle men's approval with great humility. But when most people receive even a little bit of praise or money or success, they get completely thrown off.

> The crucible is for silver, and the furnace is for gold, so a person is tested by being praised.
>
> —PROVERBS 27:21, NRSV

It's amazing how quickly success affects the human heart. Something goes crazy in people, and they swoon with intoxicating pride upon receiving even the smallest amount of earthly honor. They find themselves unable to "tend sheep" anymore. They see all the people standing in line waiting to see them, and they conclude they can no longer bother with menial jobs. They say, "I don't have time for small stuff. I'm the anointed of God." They get distracted in the swirl of new activity. They fight to uphold their new image.

The history of the human race tells us that when most people get promoted even a little, they don't become more devout. Rather, they lose their tenderness toward the Lord. They lose intimacy with Him and begin to see their identity in their ministry. That's why God warned, "Beware that you do not forget the LORD your God... lest—when you have eaten and are full, and have built beautiful houses . . . when your . . . silver and your gold are multiplied . . . when your heart is lifted up, and you forget the LORD your God" (Deut. 8:11–14).

David was a different sort. When he was promoted to Gibeah, he continued to live from his heart as he did in Bethlehem, faithful to his small responsibilities. He went back and forth between Saul's court and the hillside in Bethlehem, taking supplies to his brothers who were in Saul's army and then returning home to take care of the sheep (1 Sam. 17:15, 18, 22). Though he was beginning to taste the favor and esteem of men, he continued to be faithful in insignificant tasks.

WHAT DAVID PROBABLY DIDN'T KNOW IS THAT IN ALL THIS EARLY SUCCESS, GOD WAS TESTING THE CHARACTER OF HIS LOVE AND SERVANTHOOD.

What was his secret? He was not on a quest for success and importance because he already had it in being loved by God. He had learned the lesson of Bethlehem, and not even the success of Gibeah shook him from it. David declared, "O LORD, You brought my soul up from the grave; You have kept me alive, that I should not go down to the pit. . . . Now in my prosperity I said, 'I shall never be moved.' LORD, by Your favor You have made my mountain stand strong" (Ps. 30:3, 6–7). He was declaring that even in times of prosperity, he would not be moved. He would not give himself over to the fleeting praise of men but would anchor his soul in the Lord.

God knew this season of favor would only be temporary. He wanted David to learn to respond with humility and love whether in Bethlehem or Gibeah, isolation or the national spotlight. Often, the Lord will give us a certain amount of success to equip us for the wilderness years that are yet ahead. We will suddenly find ourselves in a position of prominence or leadership where people value our time and opinions. We will feel an amazing rush from all the attention. People will praise us in private and in public. We will receive the applause of men. But that's never the end of the story. Life alternates between times of promotion and times of struggle, times of favor and times of difficulty. Most people never imagine that the season of success will change, but it almost always does. No season continues unbroken in life. As we journey forward, the prosperity and favor of men will come and go, and in the end they're not worth much. But when we learn how to lean on Him alone in times of success, we will know how to find Him in times of difficulty.

The lesson of Gibeah is that promotion comes not from the east, west, or south but from the north—from the Lord (Ps. 75:6–7). He encourages us to not be swept up in the temporary favor or persecution of men. This divine training process is on display all throughout Scripture. Remember Moses, who was the head of Pharaoh's house and one of the leaders in Egypt. He had great authority when he was forty years old. He must have thought the hard years were over. Yet the Lord had a different plan. He moved Moses from prominence to the wilderness for forty years. Then He raised him up again and made him one of the greatest men of all history.

Joseph too experienced early promotion and demotion. He received favor from his father, but that got him in trouble with his ten older brothers. He was sold as a slave to the Egyptians, then found himself over the whole guard in Potiphar's house. He may have thought all the promises were coming to pass and he was on the permanent high road, but there was another dungeon ahead. He was sent to prison for a number of years. Finally he was entrusted with all the wealth of Egypt.

Still another man of God experienced this seesaw of success and difficulty. Saul of Tarsus, who would become the apostle Paul, had a supernatural encounter with Jesus on the way to Damascus (Acts 9). The whole Christian world was talking about this new convert. But after his immediate international success, he spent at least fourteen years in the desert without anything happening in his ministry. Then, for a while, he had a successful healing and evangelism ministry, but then it was off to prison and beatings and death.

Each man in these examples learned to find his identity in God in the character-testing time of early success. That's what we learn from David's years in Gibeah. Have you tasted success? Did you realize your character was being tested? God wants you to establish your identity fully in Him and learn to handle the favor of men in the same way you handled the obscurity. If you pass the test, you "graduate" to the next season—though you may wish you hadn't.

> WHEN WE LEARN HOW TO LEAN ON HIM ALONE IN TIMES OF SUCCESS, WE WILL KNOW HOW TO FIND HIM IN TIMES OF DIFFICULTY.

Adullam: The Cave of Difficulty

> David left Gath and escaped to the cave of Adullam.... All those who were in distress or in debt or discontented gathered around him, and he became their leader. About four hundred men were with him.
>
> —1 SAMUEL 22:1–2, NIV

After the praises and promotion in Gibeah, David's career took a sharp turn. He lost all favor in Saul's court. Instantly, the outward trappings of success fell away. His fame and popularity had created a raft of jealous enemies who now emerged with knives drawn. Saul rose up to kill him and enlisted three thousand men to chase, capture, and murder him. They were each given a salary, food, and transportation, all for the purpose of killing him. Seldom has there been such a dramatic reversal. David, probably confused and exasperated, at least initially, fled and made his headquarters in the dark, damp wilderness cave of Adullam. There he gathered four hundred men together, and for about seven years they and their families wandered the wilderness.

This was the complete opposite of the lifestyle he had grown accustomed to in the king's court in Gibeah. He lived exposed to the elements, sleeping wherever nature afforded him a decent bed. He had to worry about food and water. There were no servants like in Saul's court: no living quarters, no cooks. He couldn't just blend in because everybody in the nation knew who he was. He was marked for death. Spies tracked him and told Saul of his whereabouts. God slammed the brakes on David's early success, rammed it into reverse gear, and took him into one of the toughest times imaginable.

Gibeah had tested him with praise and success. Now Adullam was testing him with hardship. This was no fairy-tale season of sanitized suffering. It was touch-and-go, with lives hanging in the balance. God's promises appeared distant and faint. David became truly discouraged a few times and concluded they would never come to pass. He said in his heart, "Now I shall perish someday by the hand of Saul" (1 Sam. 27:1). He complained, cried, screamed, threw temper tantrums, and quit a couple of times. He never quit in the long term, but he was overcome with discouragement for months at a stretch. At times he said, "God, just kill me. I'm not going to be a king anyway." Then he would repent of his wrong attitudes and say, "OK, I'm going to follow You with all my heart. You win again." He was often mad, hurt, and despairing. And who wouldn't be?

God put David in Adullam for seven long years to firmly root his identity in God. The lessons of this season, though extremely difficult to learn, would prove to be his protection when he became king of Israel. In the same way, God doesn't want us to get our identity even a little bit from our anointing or earthly success but from being loved by God and being a lover of God. Our ministry can fall apart. The people who admired us can leave. The blessing of the Spirit can lift off our labors for a season. We can lose our building, our home, and our financial base, but if we love God and He loves us, we are still successful. This is the sure inheritance the Father has promised us.

If we are to become people after God's own heart, it's important that we remain so in tune with God's reality that we encounter Him in good times without becoming proud and in bad times without giving up. We must remember when we suddenly are shoved into an Adullam season that God has a divine pattern for maturing us. Wilderness seasons can cause great confusion. It appears as though the plan of God for our life has changed. Yet in truth, God has only changed our season, not our purpose or destiny. Those are firm in Him. Our only job is to pass the test of the season we're in.

David's difficult congregation

Adullam was tough for another reason as well. The people who gathered to David were not exactly Israel's best and brightest. Their spiritual roots were not deeply anchored in God. They were not four hundred people overflowing in God and ready to serve with joy. On the contrary, they were in distress, in debt, and discontented with Saul and the government. We might think of them as the losers of society, the guys who got into scrapes and fights and legal tangles. Some of them were outlaws who were emotionally and financially immature. The rest were burned out, stressed out, angry, and wounded. They came to David and said, "Take care of us. It's time somebody else thinks for me!"

This sounds like a lot of churches today who are camped out at Adullam. Their people collapse when things don't go right. They get blindsided by the changing season. They have a hard time holding on to God when things go wrong. The great news is that these men were transformed from a needy group of people to become the mighty men of David by the end of the story.

THE LORD WILL ACTUALLY TEST YOU WITH THE OPPOSITE OF WHAT HE PLANS TO GIVE YOU IN THE TIME OF BLESSING.

In Adullam, God taught David a dual lesson about his own sin and weakness as well as the sins and the weaknesses of those who joined him. When David had Saul at the end of a spear, his men counseled, "Kill him! The word of the Lord said you would triumph over him. Go ahead and use that sword of yours." David responded, "He's the Lord's anointed. I can't kill him." They gave him bad advice because they didn't see God as David's source, but David saw differently. That's why he was king. He ruled his soul. He understood that there are times to disagree with people around you for the sake of obeying God.

Idealism and naiveté about relationships are removed from us in Adullam. This is the place where we discover that God is real and He alone is our supply even in greatest distress, not the people He sends our way. Many Christians go from one disappointment to another because they put too much stock in relationships with the people God puts in their lives. They shift their sense of success to their valued friendships or how well they work with people, and this leads to making decisions based on the opinions of people around them. This is an easy deception to fall into, especially in the body of Christ where we place such a high value on each individual. But in times of hardship we learn to rule our spirit, as the Bible says. We get so anchored in God that if everything collapses and everyone turns against us, we say as David said, "I will bless the LORD at all times. His praise shall continually be in my mouth" (Ps. 34:1). We learn to subject ourselves entirely to God's will, not man's opinions.

> Whoever has no rule over his own spirit is like a city broken down, without walls.
>
> —PROVERBS 25:28

The good news of Adullam is that it gives you hints and foreshadowing of what you can expect in the time of God's full release of your destiny. The Lord will actually test you with the opposite of what He plans to give you in the time of blessing. For example, the Lord may have in mind to bless you financially, so in the Adullam time somebody might cheat you out of $5,000. The way to pass that test and season is to recognize that all your money belongs to the Lord since He is your source. When you settle that issue, you view money differently. You place your identity in Him, not in your checkbook. You are prepared for prosperity.

The same principle applies with being criticized. If criticism hurts you, then praise will affect you negatively as well. Both criticism and praise are invitations to find your identity in opinions of people. If you can handle all the conflicting opinions, the critics, and the flatterers without changing your opinion of yourself and God, you will be prepared to move on. Or consider the anointing of God on ministries. If you can't be faithful without the manifest anointing on your ministry, then you certainly won't be faithful with it. You will get excited, take things into your own hands, and cause a lot of harm.

So the struggles you are visited with in Adullam turn out to be training for the way God wants to bless you in Zion. In your time of deepest struggle you will see hints of what's to come in your life. But don't be too hasty. Another season lies between you and the place of your destiny.

Hebron: The Beginnings of the Prophetic Purpose

> In the course of time, David inquired of the LORD. "Shall I go up to one of the towns of Judah?" he asked. The LORD said, "Go up." David asked, "Where shall I go?" "To Hebron," the LORD answered.
>
> —2 SAMUEL 2:1, NIV

After approximately seven difficult years in the wilderness, the season finally changed with the death of King Saul. David came out of the desert at about thirty years of age. Upon hearing of Saul's death, his first response might have been, "At last, I can be king over all Israel!" His men jumped to this assumption. They cried with a sense of relief, "David! You're finally king. Let's move in." But in this key moment, David did something surprising. Instead of agreeing with his men, he responded, "Maybe God doesn't want me to be king of Israel in this season. Let me ask the Lord first."

WE MUST SENSE IN OUR SPIRITS AND DISCERN IF AN OPEN DOOR IS OF GOD OR IF IT LEADS DOWN A FALSE PATH.

This possibility was almost too painful to consider. His men might have said, "What do you mean? God has spoken it, Saul is out of the way, and you've been waiting for nearly thirteen years since the prophet Samuel anointed you." But David did the unexpected thing. He sought God's heart. He demonstrated what people who are intimate with God do before making big decisions. He asked the Lord if he should go up to live in any of the cities of Judah instead of going straight to Gibeah to replace Saul. He prayed one of the great prayers in his life, "Shall I go up?"—meaning, should he go up to Gibeah to replace Saul as king. The Lord answered him and told him to go up to Hebron instead.

That answer disappointed David's men. Going up to Hebron meant David was only taking about a twelfth of the kingdom Saul had governed. David could have agreed with all those around him and interpreted the death of Saul as the indication that God had made a way for him to be king over all Israel, but he left room for the voice of God. An open door in the natural stood before him, but he refused to enter it without the direct leading of the Lord. Beloved, this is how we must behave! We must never think we can advance willy-nilly without seeking the Lord's heart for a situation. Just because things seem to be falling together doesn't mean the right time has come. We must sense in our spirits and discern if an open door is of God or if it leads down a false path. The Holy Spirit will give us wisdom about this at the time of decision.

The Lord told David to go to Hebron and only take a little bit of the kingdom. There were twelve tribes of Israel, and Hebron represented only one. God was testing and training David once again. He wanted David to find his identity in God, not in being king of Israel. Therefore, God only released a partial fulfillment of the full destiny promised to him.

God will do this to us, too. It's an agonizing experience, but it builds incredible patience in us. David spent seven more years limited to the city of Hebron. Remember, at this point, he had waited to be king for thirteen or fourteen years. Still, he didn't become angry with God for making him wait through another season of testing. He knew the Lord would give him all of Israel when it was time. He was after the perfect will of God and would not settle for less. The only reason David could act this way lay in his identity: being king of Israel was not the key to his sense of importance. And we too will triumph in the lesson of Hebron when we see we are already successful before God and don't strive for success before men by going after position and honor. If this lesson first learned way back in Bethlehem isn't part of our very fiber, we may fail in this fourth season of life.

Forming the team

One reason God gave David only one-twelfth of the kingdom in Hebron was because He wanted David's core of fighting men—the future army of Israel—to become mature and seasoned. If God gets the core right, He can add the multitudes later. David's band of men had grown to about six hundred. Some formerly were independent, self-willed, stubborn, and in it for themselves. They were strong in bravery and might individually, but not strong together and not strong in the Lord. They had spent many years relying on their own brawn and skills. But God was committed to transforming them into a covenant community. He wanted a core of submitted, committed leaders free of ambition. God has no use for freelancers or mavericks, no matter how highly skilled. To their credit, these men humbled themselves and came together for the covenant purposes of God. They became loyal and unified. They became righteous warriors, using their strength for the greater glory of God and Israel

OUR OCCUPATION AND IMAGE BEFORE PEOPLE SHOULD NEVER MOTIVATE US. OUR GREATEST PRIVATE AGENDA MUST REMAIN TO BE LOVED BY GOD AND TO BE A LOVER OF GOD.

instead of doing their own thing. They found the secret that working together produces far greater results than going it alone. They became a mighty army that God used to make Israel great among the nations.

Hebron speaks to us of finding God in times of partial fulfillment of His promises. This can be a painful season in our lives. The blessing seems to come so slow. You may pass the test of isolation and obscurity in Bethlehem, the test of early promotion in Gibeah, and the test of adversity in Adullam. But many of God's servants stumble in this place represented by Hebron. Things look so ripe, so ready that they think they have passed the ultimate test. They grab hold of the situation without inquiring of God. They begin to cheat and find their identity in being a prominent, anointed servant of God. But we must keep our identities in Him even when the promises are at our very fingertips. Even in that place of tantalizing closeness, God demands a righteous response. If He is truly the primary reward of our hearts, then we will not need to be king. He could tell us to go back to Bethlehem, and we would gladly do it. Our occupation and image before people should never motivate us. Our greatest private agenda must remain to be loved by God and to be a lover of God. That's the lesson for us from David's season in Hebron.

Zion: The Promises Fulfilled

After seven years of reigning in Hebron, David was thirty-seven years old. It had been twenty years since the original prophecy that he would be king over all Israel. Now, Saul had four sons, three of whom were killed in battle with him. But one son, Ishbosheth, remained. He was not a warrior and not kingly material. He had no following among the people of Israel. All Israel knew that David was the rightful king. Nevertheless, David refused to overthrow this son of Saul, who was living at Gibeah and shaking like a leaf in fear of David. David waited for the season of God's promotion. It arrived one day when Ishbosheth was murdered by wicked men.

> All the tribes of Israel came to David.... When all the elders of Israel had come to King David at Hebron, the king made a compact with them at Hebron before the Lord, and they anointed David king over Israel.
>
> —2 SAMUEL 5:1–3, NIV

David had arrived. This season of Zion speaks to us of the full release of what God promised David during his earthly lifetime. This is when the full prophetic destiny for our lives begins to be manifest. David would soon capture Jerusalem, referred to as "Zion" in Scripture, and set up his capital there instead of Gibeah. The Bible says several things about this season:

> David went on and became great, and the LORD God of hosts was with him.
>
> —2 SAMUEL 5:10

> I have been with you wherever you have gone, and have cut off all your enemies from before you, and have made you a great name, like the name of the great men who are on the earth.
>
> —2 SAMUEL 7:9

> David knew that the LORD had established him as king over Israel, and that He had exalted His kingdom for the sake of His people Israel.
>
> —2 SAMUEL 5:12

There are several lessons for us in Zion. The first is this: there is no substitute for the confidence we feel upon arriving at our destiny in God's time and in His way. David knew God had made him king. He didn't cheat along the journey or claim the kingship by force. He didn't kill Saul or negotiate with Abner or overthrow Ishbosheth. He didn't manipulate or prod anyone to come down to Hebron and make him king. So when he did become king over all Israel, he felt totally secure. He could relax. He could lie down on his bed and take a nap and not worry about keeping the kingdom in his control. Being king was God's idea, not David's. David didn't have to keep his position by strife and manipulation.

Many people work hard to get their ministry moving and happening. They strive at work to attain a certain position. But sometimes they feel God hasn't moved fast enough on their behalf, so they hurry it along with unholy manipulation. They may get the position or prominence they want, but they lack any confidence in it. They are consumed with fear that somebody will take over their territory or steal their position. They live with anxiety because they can't be sure God gave the ministry or position to them in the first place. They have built on a faulty foundation. Beloved, I exhort you for the sake of your purpose and destiny in this life, allow God to take you to your Zion! Don't step out of line; don't rush. There is no second best in this. You either arrive legitimately with the confidence of heaven behind you, or you arrive illegitimately and riddled with anxiety.

> THERE IS NO SUBSTITUTE FOR THE CONFIDENCE WE FEEL UPON ARRIVING AT OUR DESTINY IN GOD'S TIME AND IN HIS WAY.

The second lesson is: God doesn't bring us to Zion for our personal enrichment. Often the Lord's blessing will rest on a person, congregation, nation, or city, and they start thinking the blessing was given mostly to add to their personal prestige or lifestyle. They think their success is a testimony to their strength of character rather than to the extraordinary grace of God. This is a danger we must avoid once we arrive at our destiny. David knew God had chosen him for the sake of the people. The Lord didn't mind blessing David in the process, but His ultimate purpose in bringing him to Zion was to bless others, not to give him a lifestyle of the rich and famous. Arriving at Zion is about serving the kingdom in greater measure—a privilege far greater than money or fame.

Third, some people imagine that when they finally reach the fullness of their promise and place of destiny, they will have only joy. They picture complete contentment in their anointing and prominence. But it doesn't work that way, even in the grace of God. In our place of destiny, we will still experience pressures, persecutions, and pain. People can be very naïve about how happy they will be when they finally receive an anointing that makes their ministry or business large and successful. I know several men in their sixties who have very large ministries. God is releasing the fullness of everything He has ever promised them. But each man has the same testimony: "It's not nearly as exciting as I thought it would be. In fact, it's much more difficult than I imagined." They speak to crowds of thousands all over the world. They see many people saved and healed by the power of God. But when they leave the stage, the only real satisfaction comes from being loved by God and loving Him back. This is true of those whom God prospers in the marketplace, too. When all the honor and money come, they still only find security, success, and peace in God. As you prepare to enter your destiny, set your expectations correctly.

THE LORD WILL NOT ALLOW ANY KIND OF ANOINTING OR MANDATE TO TAKE THE PLACE OF THE ULTIMATE SATISFACTION OF LOVING HIS SON.

The fourth lesson is that Zion is a prophetic picture of Jesus being made King over all the earth just as David was king over all Israel. It would be a shame to miss this beautiful portrait of what's coming. The Father has promised His Son an inheritance, a bride who will be His eternal partner. She will love Him in this age and the age to come. She will find her fulfillment in Him just as David found fulfillment of his earthly purpose in Zion.

Those are the five seasons you go through as God equips you to be a person after His heart, fulfilling your individual and corporate destiny. You start in Bethlehem, where you have an appointment with the small things. If you can clean the toilets there and feel wonderful fulfillment in the love of God, you are on the road of preparation. If you no longer find God in servanthood, you will be stuck in Bethlehem a long time. Second, the Lord will often give you a little success and blessing to test your heart at the beginning of your ministry, as He did David at Gibeah. With early success you may pray, "Lord, I am now ready to take over Billy Graham's mantle." The Lord says, "No, I'm showing you your heart so I can prepare you for the years to come." Next, the Lord takes you through the season of testing and negative circumstances near the cave of Adullam. When you pass this test, you might again think you have arrived, but God moves you to Hebron, where He gives you only one-twelfth of your promised destiny. He establishes and matures you until you are ready for Zion. Seven years later, figuratively speaking, the fullness comes. Yet even in the joy of fullness, there is still a groan in your spirit. The Lord will not allow any kind of anointing or mandate to take the place of the ultimate satisfaction of loving His Son.

David wrote:

> Blessed are those whose strength is in you, who have set their hearts on pilgrimage. As they pass through the Valley of Baca, they make it a place of springs; the autumn

> rains also cover it with pools. They go from strength to strength, till each appears before God in Zion.
>
> —Psalm 84:5–7

God has a prophetic pilgrimage for every one of us. All of us are at different levels of maturity and in different seasons. But like David, we can go through times of weeping, going from spring to spring and strength to strength. At the end of our story we will come up out of the wilderness, out of Adullam, leaning on the Lord's breast as John did at the Last Supper. We will be like the bride portrayed in Song of Solomon at the end of her story as one victorious in love, leaning tenaciously upon her Bridegroom King. "Who is this that cometh up from the wilderness, leaning upon her beloved?" (Song of Sol. 8:5, KJV). She had no certainty in her own heart and motives. She trusted only in the Lord.

I want to assure you that there's a divine pattern in your life. In the pain and the maze of things, it seems as if there isn't a plan and you are wandering aimlessly from cave to cave, pursued by armies much stronger than you, and surrounded by losers. Yet God has a strategic plan and is bringing you to a specific purpose. Each one of us will, God willing, stand before Him one day in Zion. When we submit to His divine leadership in every season of our lives, we will ascend out of the wilderness entirely dependent on Him. He alone will be the reward of our hearts through every season of life.

I want to pair this study with a profound lesson we learn from David that will help us through each of these seasons. It was such a powerful truth that Jesus repeated it as He hung on the cross. The seven words will help us through the darkest times of our journey.

12

Chapter Twelve

"INTO YOUR HANDS I COMMIT MY SPIRIT"

You may wonder how David made it through the obstacle course of opposition on the way to Zion and his destiny. It may seem impossible to follow that example. But there is a truth that empowered him the entire way, and if you can discover and hold to it even in the worst seasons, you will make it to the end, too. In fact, this truth is so powerful that it was among the last words of Jesus.

Luke wrote in his Gospel: "Now it was about the sixth hour, and there was darkness over all the earth" (Luke 23:44). Jesus' broken body hung on the cross, moments before His final breath. Darkness loomed over the soul of the God-Man as He who knew no sin became sin. The sun was blackened, and the veil of the temple was about to be torn. Jesus felt the agony of separation from the Father. He knew that on the other side of the agony was the awesome promise that God would raise Him from the dead and enthrone Him over all created order. But before the fullness of the promise came to pass, He experienced the greatest pressure and opposition any man has faced. In that dark delay, what came forth from Son of Man's heart? What words expressed His deepest soul? He went back to the words of King David from Psalm 31:5, lifted His voice, and cried out, "Into Your hands I commit My Spirit" (Luke 23:46). Jesus decided this was the most appropriate heart response He could have while waiting for the light and promise to break forth. Then He said, "It is finished!" and breathed His last (John 19:30). And it was over.

When God gives a promise, we usually experience a time of darkness before He brings it to pass. Often in these times, we experience the silence of God and the opposition of man, as David did. The prophetic promises of God seem clouded by every kind of fear and trouble. We have a hard time seeing what season we're in or where it's all leading. In the hour of the impossible situation, what should you do? Grab hold of those seven words, and commit your spirit into the Father's hands.

Committing Our Spirit to God

What does it mean to commit our spirits to the Lord? Our spirit is the part of us that touches our deepest desires and dreams. It is the repository for our greatest passions and hopes for our lives. As He hung on the cross, Jesus was saying, "Father, I commit to You the things I treasure the most. I surrender to Your hand what I have lived for and believed in." I believe Jesus was declaring the secret of how He lived His entire earthly life. At the end of His life He knew this spiritual principle would again prove reliable and true. God was His source, and God is our source. Committing our spirits to Him means asking the Father to take care of those things that matter most to our hearts. It is recognizing that we can't make God's promises come to pass in our own strength.

In Psalm 31:4, the verse before "Into Your hand...," David said, "Pull me out of the net which they have secretly laid for me."

The net can represent many things to us, like spiritual, physical, financial, or relational quagmires. In Jesus' experience, the net was His bearing the sin of the world before His exaltation. He cried, "Father, pull Me out of the impossible situation, for You are My strength." He knew He could not deliver Himself as He hung in the dark place between promise and fulfillment. His confidence rested in His Father alone. He was suffering the greatest injustice any man has ever suffered, and He harkened back to the reality David had declared when he was dealing with his own injustice. "Into Your hands I commit my spirit." In our own times of trouble and personal injustice, the Lord is looking for that same cry to come forth from our hearts. Beloved, in our difficult seasons of life, we must commit our deepest passions and prophetic promises to God. God is calling us to this place of dependence. He is beckoning us to depend on Him with every hope for breakthrough, every need for provision, every dream of success. We must surrender our deepest desires to God's keeping. We are utterly unable to bring our prophetic promises to pass. Only He can change the times and seasons and bring the breakthrough we long for.

> COMMITTING OUR SPIRITS TO HIM MEANS ASKING THE FATHER TO TAKE CARE OF THOSE THINGS THAT MATTER MOST TO OUR HEARTS.

When you commit something into God's hands, the devil cannot steal it. Just as Saul could not stop the will of God in David's life, no outside force will stop you. The only person who could stop the will of God in David's life was David. And only you can stop God's will from happening in your life by disconnecting from communion with God. When our spirits are hidden in Him, the enemy can't lay a finger on them. The prophetic dream of our heart is kept alive. The apostle Peter talked about this when he wrote that Jesus "entrusted himself to him [God] who judges justly" (1 Pet. 2:23, NIV). He meant that Jesus looked to God to spare Him when the Pharisees were trying to kill Him before His time.

David lived this way, and it set him apart from so many others. He had a tremendous tenacity to take what he cared most about and thrust it into the realm of God's activity. Time and again he pressed his very being into God's care, transferring his entire self with all his anxieties, opinions, passions, and dreams into the hands of God. When David said, "I commit my spirit," he surrendered to the Lord all that went into making him a man after God's own heart. He said, "I want my life to be lost in the realm of God's activity and intervention." He wanted to understand his life through God's actions, not his own.

In our fallenness, we often commit our spirits to what others say about us. We make the mistake of seeing our values and dreams in the hands of the people around us. When they don't appreciate us, our dreams and sense of importance seem jeopardized. Some people commit their spirits into the hands of powerful leaders in the secular and Christian world, thinking if they find favor with that leader, their destiny will finally be accomplished. But when we live this way, we live in turmoil. Why? Because that leader may withhold the blessing. Or he or she might give the blessing only to take it away later. Any man or woman, no matter how great, is an unsure place to commit our spirits. The key is to commit our deepest dreams and desires to God.

WHEN WE STAND BEFORE GOD IN ETERNITY, WE WILL REALIZE HE WAS NEVER ONE MINUTE LATE.

In Psalm 31:15, David said, "My times are in Your hand." It's one thing to commit our spirits into God's hands; it's quite another thing to trust God with the timing of His breakthrough. Each "committing" has its own challenges and anxieties. After we commit our spirits into God's hands, the test of time comes. One year turns into two, and two years turn into ten. We begin to question, "What about the breakthrough? What about the promises?" Though we have committed our spirits to Him, the years have multiplied. David saw there were two steps to this. First, he committed his spirit; then he committed the timing of those dreams. He learned to rest in God's sovereignty. We too must give ourselves to this two-part progression. First, we commit our spirits and dreams into God's hands by living lives of prayer and fasting as we seek their fulfillment. Second, we trust Him for the season of release. When we stand before God in eternity, we will realize He was never one minute late.

Spiritual Warfare: Bringing God Into Our Conflicts

Committing our spirits into God's hands is an act of aggressive spiritual warfare, not passive indifference. David did it to bring God into his conflicts. He wasn't kicking back and saying, "Whatever happens, happens; I really don't care, Lord." No, he was using a spiritual tactic to bring God into the situation of his personal injustice. He engaged in this kind of spiritual warfare from his youth to the end of his life. When he entrusted a specific situation to God, there was a reaction and a release in the spirit realm. God moved on David's behalf. David became a model of how God settles the score when we war according to His way.

When Joseph faced his brothers after having suffered years of injustice because of their initial decision to sell him into slavery, he could have said, "Ha! I told you I would rule over you." But as he stood before them in his position of power and honor, he had no desire to settle the score or have the last word. He was lost in the kindness of God. In the same way, the Lord realigns our emotions and motives through our individual training process. We learn in a thousand times and ways to say, "Into Your hands I commit my spirit." As we work that faith muscle, it equips our hearts to receive the blessing and intervention of God. He brings us into His likeness. He beckons us to enter His heart and leave the agenda of justice to Him.

> EVERY TIME SOMEONE HARMS YOU, IT'S ANOTHER DIVINE OPPORTUNITY TO SHOUT TO THE WORLD THAT THE LORD OWNS YOU AND WILL DEFEND YOU ACCORDING TO HIS RIGHTEOUSNESS.

One key characteristic in David's life was the way he processed pain, mistreatment, disappointment, and injustice, a process recorded so richly in the Book of Psalms. He learned to war in the spirit by giving up his right to revenge. Other men and women of God such as Daniel, Joseph, and the patriarchs of old operated in this principle as well. Paul put it this way:

> Repay no one evil for evil.... Beloved, do not avenge yourselves, but rather give place to wrath; for it is written, "Vengeance is Mine, I will repay," says the Lord. Therefore "If your enemy is hungry, feed him; if he is thirsty, give him a drink; for in so doing you will heap coals of fire on his head." Do not be overcome by evil, but overcome evil with good.
>
> —ROMANS 12:17–21

Vengeance belongs in God's hands. He settles scores perfectly. When we place the injustice done to us in God's hands, we allow room for His vengeance. If we act in an angry spirit and try to vindicate ourselves, God steps back and lets us fight alone. His plan is that He takes revenge however He sees fit, and we bless our enemy even as He works vengeance. He is a God who mostly wants to bless and be merciful, and as we bless our enemies, we exhibit His character even as He doles out justice. That's His idea for showing mercy even when justice is needed. Jesus said it best:

> But I say to you who hear: Love your enemies, do good to those who hate you, bless those who curse you, and pray for those who spitefully use you.... But love your enemies, do good, and lend, hoping for nothing in return; and your reward will be great, and you will be sons of the Most High. For He is kind to the unthankful and evil.
>
> —Luke 6:27–35

When we are kind to our enemies, we mirror the Father's kindness for evil and ungrateful men, and we come into unity with the Ruler of the universe. There is no form of spiritual warfare more powerful than that.

When you want to retaliate, remember that the fundamental reality in the kingdom of God is 1 Corinthians 6:19–20, "Do you not know that...you are not your own? For you were bought at a price;...in your body and in your spirit, which are God's." Beloved, when you show kindness to your enemies, it declares you belong to another. Your resources belong to God, your reputation belongs to Him, and your time belongs to Him. When your enemies bring pressure on you, malign your reputation, or steal your resources or your time, the Lord invites you to make a transfer of ownership and put your complete self into His hands. This makes room for His vengeance and His agenda. He is your Defense and your Ally. If He is not concerned to immediately punish the injustice done to you, then neither should you be worried—you belong to Him. This is the path to true liberty and true power. Every time someone harms you, it's another divine opportunity to shout to the world that the Lord owns you and will defend you according to His righteousness.

When David was young, Saul gave him plenty of opportunity to practice this type of spiritual warfare. In later years, David faced a rebellious young prince who tried to rip the kingdom away from him. In both of these conflicts, David responded rightly. He learned to commit his spirit into God's hands. Therefore, when men moved in around him to challenge his standing or take away his position, his soul remained at peace. But we can learn from one of his most severe tests, which he experienced after many years as king. After a lifetime of bringing God into his conflicts, David found that his son had made himself David's enemy. Let's look at a few scenes from this sad time as David tried to choose God's way in the pit of painful testing.

The Resolve to Remain in God's Hands

Saul and Absalom act almost like bookends on David's life. Both were rebellious before God. Both sought David's life. Both worked ruthlessly to make and hold a position God had not granted or had taken away. Second Samuel 15:1–2 tells us:

> After this it happened that Absalom provided himself with chariots and horses, and fifty men to run before him. Now Absalom would rise early and stand beside the way to the gate.

Absalom would get up early and stand beside the gate of the city. As people came from other parts of the kingdom with their lawsuits and complaints, Absalom called out to them to sway their hearts toward him. He would say things like, "Your case is good and right. Too bad my father doesn't have enough staff to take care of it. If I were the king, I would treat you better than that." After speaking with them, he would kiss their hand with false affection and say, "Say hi to the wife and kids when you go home." He stole the hearts of Israel away from David by smooth talk and betrayal, and it worked. The people began to gravitate toward him.

When he was ready, Absalom lied to David and said he was going to Hebron to pay a vow to the Lord (2 Sam. 15:7). Instead, Absalom went there to rally his men for a revolution. He sent his recruits through Hebron with a trumpet announcement, saying, "Absalom is king in Hebron!" The conspiracy was born, and news came to David that "the hearts of the men of Israel are with Absalom in Hebron" (v. 13). Though David had led this nation in the way of godliness for so many years, a significant number in the army of Israel defected from him for the chance of a promotion with Absalom. They were willing to abandon the prophetic destiny of David and Israel for the chance to strike it rich quick with a new young king.

The nation was in crisis. Half the people were with David, and half were with Absalom. In 2 Samuel 15:14, we find King David gathering his personal servants to flee Jerusalem. David knew that if he and his men didn't leave, Jerusalem would be engulfed in bloodshed when Absalom arrived with his army. All the country wept with a loud voice as David crossed the Brook Kidron toward the way of the wilderness, not knowing even where he was going (v. 23).

As they fled, Zadok the priest approached David to help. Zadok brought the ark of the covenant so they would win the battle against Absalom. I imagine he ran up breathless and said, "Good news; I have the ark of the covenant. Now victory is assured."

David responded, in essence, "Guys, carry the ark back. We don't need to twist God's arm to get Him to help us. He owns everything, and I know He likes me and has the best in mind for me. What I need right now is not a blessed piece of furniture but a living connection with His heart. If the Lord wants me to be king, then I will be king, and He will bring me back" (v. 25). By this time in his life, David was drawing on a lifetime of committing his spirit to God in times of crisis. He had exercised this faith muscle so much it was becoming second nature. He answered Zadok, "But if He [God] says thus: 'I have no delight in you,' *here I am*, let Him do to me as seems good to Him" (v. 26, emphasis added). It was as if he threw open his arms before God and said, "I am the Lord's! I belong to Him! He can do what He wants with me."

God's ability to retain David as king was not in question. Yet with a sincere heart David welcomed the possibility that God might not desire him to be king anymore. He allowed that the Lord, in His mysterious administration, was saying it was time for a new king. God had never promised he would be king forever. If it was his time to step down, David didn't mind.

Still running from Absalom, David and his men came to the town of Bahurim (2 Sam. 16:5). As they neared the town, an enemy named Shimei came out cursing him. Shimei was a bitter old leader from Saul's regime. Saul was long dead, but resentment was alive and well in Shimei's heart. His anger flaring out of him, Shimei cursed David and threw stones at him (v. 6). He took full advantage of David's being on the run. Some of David's mighty men were standing next to David. With one syllable, David could have commanded them to annihilate the man for his disloyalty. Just as Jesus in Matthew 26:53 could have called a legion of angels to wipe out His accusers, all David would have had to do was nod, and this man would have been killed. Yet with all the resources of his loyal army in his reach, David remained silent.

Shimei sneered, "Come out of your hiding, you bloodthirsty

man, you rogue!" He brought a prophetic curse on David, saying, "The Lord has brought all of the bloodshed of Saul on you because you are a bloodthirsty man. You mistreated Saul, taking the throne from him and reigning in his place. Now you are caught in your own evil, and the Lord has delivered the kingdom into Absalom's hand. Thus says the Lord, He has shown me that you will die and your son will reign." (See 2 Samuel 16:7–8.)

Undoubtedly, David's men were saying, "That is not true. We were with you in the days of Saul." As Shimei continued to curse, one of the top generals, Abishai, said, "I can't take it anymore. Why should this dead dog curse my lord the king? Let me take this guy's head off right now!"

David responded, "What have I to do with you? Let him curse me. So what? It doesn't hurt me. Maybe God is in it. Maybe the Lord is testing me with an opportunity to wait for divine intervention."

DAVID HAD EXERCISED THIS FAITH MUSCLE SO MUCH IT WAS BECOMING SECOND NATURE.

David knew this might be a divine opportunity to choose God's way over man's, to bring God into the conflict, and to release divine power into the circumstance. So he waited on the breakthrough. He was not preoccupied with man's opinions or preserving his reputation. He wanted God and angels moving, not men wagging their tongues back and forth. David answered, "It may be that the Lord will look on my affliction, and . . . repay me with good for his cursing this day" (v. 12). David held out for the chance that God had a bigger purpose.

In 2 Samuel 18, the national crisis came to a climax. It was time for David to take care of the rebellious uprising. He commanded his top generals, "Deal gently for my sake with the young man Absalom" (v. 5). Though Absalom had stolen the hearts of the people and sought to take his own father's life and throne, David's main concern was mercy. Only a man who had spent a lifetime gazing upon God's mercy and kindness could react this way. He had experienced the Lord's mercy for years. It had begun to permeate his soul. One of my favorite verses about David is Psalm 18:35, from when David was thirty years old and coming out of his own wilderness. He wrote, "Your gentleness has made me great." What a great recognition of God's active mercy! He was saying, "I blew it so many times, and You were so gentle with me in my youth." He knew God could have canceled his life for his many weaknesses. Now, all these years later, he saw another young man blowing it, and his response was, "Lord, be gentle to Absalom. Generals, be gentle to Absalom." I believe he was saying, "Be gentle just as the Lord was gentle with me." His response was of another order and from another world.

BELOVED, WHEN YOU KNOW THAT GOD HAS GIVEN YOU A SPECIFIC ASSIGNMENT, THOUGH IT BE GREAT OR SMALL, YOU HAVE PEACE AND CONFIDENCE.

That same day Absalom was killed in battle, breaking his father's heart. After the treason was stopped and the whole kingdom restored back to David, Shimei, the man who had cursed David, came to him and repented (2 Sam. 19:19–20). David's general Abishai responded, "Should we not put this man to death for cursing the Lord's anointed?" He wanted David to take vengeance into his own hands.

> And David said, "What have I to do with you . . . that you should be adversaries to me today?" . . . Therefore

the king said to Shimei, "You shall not die." And the king swore to him.

—2 SAMUEL 19:21–23

David essentially said, "If I receive your council and act with an angry spirit, then you will have helped me miss out on God's blessing. You have become like an adversary to me. Don't you know that the whole economy of God gets short-circuited if I enter into that revengeful spirit? Has not the Lord Himself brought me back to Jerusalem as king?" Having said this, David turned to the man who cursed him and said with compassion, "You will not die. I will keep my commitment to be good to you."

The only way David made it through that horrible episode with Absalom was by continually committing his spirit to the Father. It was never his agenda to protect his throne. "David knew the LORD had established him as king over Israel" (2 Sam. 5:12). Beloved, when you know that God has given you a specific assignment, though it be great or small, you have peace and confidence. You have found the place of freedom. Your life is about God Himself, not being king over any kingdom or business or ministry or group of people. You will gladly give those up to pursue the heart of God wherever it may lead.

God wants to train us in this same spiritual warfare David excelled in, which is a significant part of becoming a people after God's own heart and a vital aspect of contending for the fullness of God's power. But sometimes it's more difficult to commit your spirit into God's hands when you've failed. Let's see how David masterfully handled those circumstances so that we don't disqualify ourselves in our own times of failure.

Chapter Thirteen

DIVINE CONTINGENCY FOR HUMAN WEAKNESS

David faced many external enemies, but he also triumphed over a much more formidable foe: his own heart. He knew how to commit his spirit into God's hands when confronted by his own weakness. This is one of the hardest things to figure out in the Christian walk, but to be people after God's heart, we must. The glory of the human story is that we can't exhaust God's mercy. Our weakness *never disqualifies* us if we sincerely repent. David discovered that there is a contingency for human weakness, which comes to us by God's grace. In his times of weakness, he ran toward God instead of away from Him.

I have taught about the life of David for more than twenty-five years, and I can find no recorded testimony in Scripture of a person more profoundly weak and also great in God. His story is filled with victory after victory alongside one weakness after another. I remember one time compiling ten sins committed by David and preaching them in one sermon. The congregation that

Sunday was horrified. They decided they didn't like David anymore. They voted to censor him out of the children's church curriculum. Not really, but they were surprised at his number of failures. I too felt like saying to David as I read about his life, "Hello! Don't you get it? You can't keep blowing it like this." Yet I imagine the Lord's response to me is, "No, don't you get it? Learn from this guy! If he can make it, so can you." Maybe when I meet David in heaven he will be mad at me for preaching so many sermons that highlight his failures. He may say, "The Lord forgave me. Why did you keep bringing those things up?" I'll say, "Because we were so much like you that your life encouraged us."

The Place of Compromise

After the season of Gibeah, you recall that David's time of favor came to a quick close, and he ran from the king's palace fearing for his life. He questioned the great prophecies over his life. He doubted his life would be spared. Saul raised up three thousand "green berets" to assassinate him, and David found himself in serious danger. Because of the weight of fear, he devised a plan of escape. But instead of running to God, he ran to the *enemy* camp seeking refuge from jealous Saul's wrath. He was afraid to stay in Israel because he doubted God's protection over him. He was so terrified that he actually decided he would be safer in Philistine territory. Imagine our great warrior king fleeing his homeland in fear! He knew Saul was too cowardly to chase him across the border, so he went to Achish, the Philistine king of the neighboring nation of Gath, and sought refuge (1 Sam. 21:10). This great worshiper of God joined the enemies of Israel.

When David took his father and mother to stay with the king of Moab, the prophet Gad prophesied to him that he was to go home to Judah. In essence he said, "Go back to Israel. Do not run and hide with the Philistines or the Moabites. Go back home and trust God" (1 Sam. 22:5). But David's faith in divine protection was wavering big-time. The prophetic word from Gad didn't have the same zip as the prophetic word he had received a few years back. David had reached the end of his courage. Years earlier, when he stood before the great giant Goliath, he had tremendous faith for protection. Before that, he was fearless before the lion and the bear. But now his faith was wounded. Even though God had sent a message right to him that He would protect him, fear conquered his heart, and he doubted the promises. In the final lap of the race before God made him king, David stumbled into great compromise in the Philistine city of Ziklag, taking six hundred men with him (1 Sam. 27:2). He chose physical security outside the will of God. And to make things worse, he promised loyalty to Achish, an archenemy of Israel.

> WE HAVE LOOKED AT DAVID AS THE GREAT WORSHIPING WARRIOR KING WITH THE HEART AFTER GOD'S, BUT HERE WE SEE HIM RIDDLED WITH THE SAME FEAR, DOUBT, AND INSECURITY WE SEE IN OURSELVES.

> David said to Achish, "If I have now found favor in your eyes, let them give me a place in some town in the country, that I may dwell there...." So Achish gave him Ziklag that day.... Now the time that David dwelt in the country of the Philistines was one full year and four months.
>
> —1 SAMUEL 27:5–7

Things had to sink pretty low for the great warrior of Israel to partner up with a zealous enemy of Israel. David began to lie and deceive people in a way he had never done before. It was a sad time in his life. He and his men would go and raid the Geshurites, the Girzites, and the Amalekites, who were enemies of Israel (v. 8). Whenever he attacked them, he killed everybody so there were no witnesses to rat him out to Achish (vv. 9–11). He would burn everything and scamper back to Achish and lie about his activities, saying he had fought against Israel when in truth he was conquering the enemies of Israel. David boldly lied to Achish every time. Achish believed him, saying, "David is making Israel utterly hate him." He believed David would be loyal to him forever (v. 12).

But David lived with terrible tension inside of him. He was a man divided. On the one hand, he still had great zeal for the Lord. That's one of the reasons he and his army made raids on Israel's enemies, not just to get livestock for his men and their families (a total of about three thousand people). On the other hand, he was living in compromise and using the favor and anointing of God in a wrong way. For his entire time in Ziklag, David lived a charade, neglecting his destiny, disobeying the prophet's word, disregarding his other prophetic promises, betraying Achish with lies, and endangering his own men and their families. We have looked at David as the great worshiping warrior king with the heart after God's, but here we see him riddled with the same fear, doubt, and insecurity we see in ourselves. But something was about to happen to yank him back onto the right road with God.

When God Burns Your Ziklag

For sixteen months, David's Ziklag strategy seemed to be working, but God was about to kick the props out from under him. One day, David and his men came home and saw their city burned to the ground (1 Sam. 30:1). While they were out of town, the Amalekites had taken revenge and sacked the place, taking all the women and children captive. God allowed Ziklag to burn so David would come face-to-face with Him. It was this very trauma that caused

David to return to God and depart this period of disobedience.

Each of us, I daresay, has a city of compromise, a Ziklag to which we retreat at some point in our lives. Our Ziklag is a place of supposed refuge that empowers us to continue in disobedience. It's the place where we devise little systems that give us sinful pleasure and false comfort when God's will becomes too intense for us. It's like a cubbyhole where we escape from the realm of God's promises and retreat into the enemy's territory where we feel safer. The Lord does not reject us during these times, but He doesn't approve of our sin, either. He looks for ways to restore us, not destroy us. He devises means so that His banished ones are not expelled from Him (2 Sam. 14:14). But He almost always allows our city of compromise to be burned. If we don't come to our senses and repent during the time of grace, our place of refuge goes up in flames. The Lord put it this way on another occasion:

> Nevertheless I have a few things against you, because you allow that woman Jezebel, who calls herself a prophetess, to teach and seduce My servants to commit sexual immorality.... I gave her time to repent of her sexual immorality, and she did not repent. Indeed I will cast her into a sickbed, and those who commit adultery with her into great tribulation, unless they repent of their deeds.
>
> —Revelation 2:20–22

Ziklag's destruction amounted to an agonizing tragedy for David and his men. They knew the Amalekites were barbaric. They thought their loved ones were dead, and so these mighty warriors cried until their eyes were so swollen they could cry no more (1 Sam. 30:4). Then their tears turned to anger. The men fumed about David's lies and compromise that had brought on the disaster. They devised a plan to stone him. David, of course, was deeply distressed (v. 6). It was one of the lowest times in his entire life. He couldn't go back to Israel because he believed King Saul would kill him. Now he faced a mutiny.

But guess what? David did the *right* thing. As a result, we know what to do when our Ziklag is burned and compromise is no longer an option. In the turmoil of this moment, "David strengthened himself in the LORD his God" (1 Sam. 30:6). When everything was falling apart, the city was burning, and his men wanted to kill him, David returned to his root system. All he had now was the knowledge that God was filled with tender mercy. Either this was true, or David was finished. He looked up to heaven, knowing the Lord loved him even then. He somehow grabbed hold of the truth that God would take him back that very day. David knelt down before the Lord and said something like, "Lord, I am Yours. I recommit my life to You right now. I love You, and I know You love me. Help me, Lord."

This is one of the greatest miracles that can happen in the life of a discouraged believer. The miracle is knowing the Lord's mercy and delight so deeply that we run toward Him in our time of greatest sin. Have you awakened one morning and realized you were living in a place of compromise? Have you watched God burn your Ziklag—your place of disobedience? Perhaps it was an unhealthy friendship, a job God never wanted you to have, or some habit of sin only you knew about until it finally erupted into the open. What did you do when you realized you had nowhere to go? David knew what God was like, so he confidently approached the Lord instead of slinking away in shame. This led to his complete recovery. If you run away from God instead of to Him in time of crisis, you can't be restored, but the complete solution will be found when you run to Him.

After strengthening himself in the Lord, David immediately asked the Lord if he should pursue and overtake the Amalekite troops who had burned Ziklag. He was back to relating to God like in his former days. The Lord answered, "Pursue, for you shall surely overtake them and without fail recover all" (1 Sam. 30:8).

Can you imagine such a statement from God? It probably shocked everyone but David. God was actually going to deliver them from the mess David had caused! David and his army attacked the enemy and recovered their families and all their belongings (vv. 18–19). That very day, another miracle happened in David's life. King Saul died in a battle in the northern part of the land (1 Sam. 31:4). This brought an end to David's years of flight as a fugitive. In one day God delivered David from the place of his compromise, delivered him from jealous King Saul, and gave him power to recover all that was taken by the Amalekites. It was like a big hand wiping the chessboard clear. It had to be one of the most dramatic days in David's life.

WHEN EVERYTHING WAS FALLING APART, THE CITY WAS BURNING, AND HIS MEN WANTED TO KILL HIM, DAVID RETURNED TO HIS ROOT SYSTEM.

Posturing Our Hearts to Receive God's Mercy

The amazing thing is that God extended this mercy on the heels of sixteen months of disobedience. Psalm 18 takes us from the external features of this story into the very center of what was happening in David's heart that day. It reveals the progression in his soul and the dynamics at work inside of him. The inscription to this psalm tells us it was written on the day God delivered David from his enemies, meaning Ziklag, Achish, the Amalekites, and King Saul. This psalm reveals the response God is looking for on the day He delivers us from our compromise.

David began with, "I will love You, O LORD, my strength" (v. 1). Consider this statement in light of his circumstances. He had just repented after a major period of compromise, and on the very first day back, he cried to God, "I love You, I love You, I love You!" Undoubtedly his six hundred men were whispering, "We don't think this guy really loves God as much as he says. We've been hanging around him, and we remember his compromise." Indeed, most people in this same situation would try to punish themselves to make up for their sin. They would put themselves in the penalty box to prove to God they were worthy of being forgiven.

> I WANT TO STAND ON THE ROOFTOPS AND SHOUT THAT SAME MESSAGE: "GOD DELIVERS US BECAUSE HE LIKES US!"

Maybe you have been caught in Ziklag before. Chances are, you felt great shame and embarrassment, that you were the lowest person in the world. You probably wanted to go into hiding for a while, show God how sorry you were, and set a schedule of devotions, prayer, and church attendance to demonstrate you were a changed person. Or maybe you were like David and had the confidence to approach God right then and say, "I love You. I know You love me right now. You see the moving of my heart toward You though I am weak." If so, you're way ahead of the game!

David went on:

> He delivered me from my strong enemy, from those who hated me, for they were too strong for me. They confronted me in the day of my calamity, but the LORD was my support. He also brought me out into a broad place; He delivered me because He delighted in me.

> The LORD rewarded me according to my righteousness; according to the cleanness of my hands He has recompensed me.
>
> —PSALM 18:17–20

Did you catch the outrageous reason he said God delivered him? *"He delivered me because He delighted in me."* I want to stand on the rooftops and shout that same message: "God delivers us because He likes us!" I can imagine some of David's men saying, "This is a little too intense. God likes you? And that's why He's letting you off the hook?" But David wasn't denying his failure; he was acknowledging that God never quit desiring him the whole time he was in compromise. Amazing!

In verse 20, David made a confusing statement. He said God rewarded him according to his righteousness. In light of David's position in sin, this is puzzling. But David wasn't referencing the previous sixteen months; rather, he was talking about the occasions when he spared Saul's life when he had him at the tip of his spear (1 Sam. 24; 26). David's men were crying, "Kill him! Kill him!" But David knew God would deliver him one day, and he refused to take matters into his own hands. This was an act of spiritual warfare on David's part, and the full victory was just being manifested. This fact did not change the last sixteen months of struggle, but it was remembered by the Lord.

Later in this psalm David said to the Lord those wonderful words, "Your gentleness has made me great" (v. 35). David had a revelation of Jesus' gentleness. He knew God could have wiped him out at Ziklag, but instead He treated him with gentleness. That bolstered David's love, and it does the same for us. God wants to make each one of us great. This doesn't mean fame or fortune, necessarily, but that He makes our heart great in love toward Him. For this purpose, He will reveal Himself as gentle to us when we are in Ziklag, the place of compromise. He will restore our confidence so we run to Him in that place. Our love will grow and grow in this kind of relationship with Him.

Tears in a Bottle

Psalm 56 develops more of the insight that helped David's confidence in God's mercy. This psalm was written while David was still living in compromise. He began in verse 1, "Be merciful to me, O God, for man would swallow me up." He was saying, "Your mercy is the one thing I am sure of." He was grieving about his current disobedience.

> You number my wanderings; put my tears into Your bottle; are they not in Your book? When I cry out to You, then my enemies will turn back; this I know, because God is for me.
>
> —Psalm 56:8–9

"You number my wanderings" is an unusual thing to write while in compromise. David said to the Lord, "God, *You* know I'm wandering. You take notice of my compromises. I'm out of Your will, and my ways are not hidden from You." Neither are we hidden from Jesus when we hide out in Ziklag. We are not deceiving God when we are stuck in compromise. But after this, David reached for the gold ring of God's mercy and said, "[You] put my tears into Your bottle; are they not in Your book?" (v. 8). David knew that his tears of despair and broken dreams, his tears of disobedience for lying and resisting the prophetic word were treasured by God. David had many different kinds of emo-

WE NEED TO PUT OUR COLD HEARTS BEFORE THAT SAME FIRE OF REVELATION THAT WARMED DAVID'S HEART.

tions churning within him. His tears were of a man who had lied and not trusted the Lord. He had endangered his friends. Yet he still loved the Lord. He wanted to be wholly God's. He knew that God was scooping his tears up in His hand and storing them in His bottle because our tears of repentance are precious to God.

In this passage, we hear the true heart of David. I imagine him sitting somewhere by himself, crying, "O God, I hate disobeying You. I love You—You know that—but I'm so afraid. I know I'm disobeying the prophetic word. I know that I am telling lies and deceiving people. But I am so afraid right now." We have all been there, crying tears of repentance. Maybe one of David's men walked up to him and said, "Hey, what are you crying about?" David could have answered, "I'm stuck in compromise, yet I love God." The guy might have kicked him and said, "Get up and quit crying, you hypocrite! God doesn't want to hear your blubbering. If you really loved God, you would stop sinning and go back to Israel like He commanded. Obey God or shut up." Yet in this moment, the Lord whispered in David's ear, "I have captured every one of your tears and put them in My bottle in heaven." David knew his tears were not despised by God; they were precious. Though the men around him likely thought he was a hypocrite, God saw genuine love in David's heart. David wrote further, "When I cry out to You, then my enemies will turn back; this I know, because God is for me" (v. 9). David believed that God was for him while he was in Ziklag, and this was the secret to his recovery.

Beloved, would you like to understand God's heart as David did? To know deeply God's heart of mercy when you are trying to get out of the sticky slough of compromise? We need to put our cold hearts before that same fire of revelation that warmed David's heart. Then, within our struggles, we will cry out with this same assurance, "I know that God is for me!"

David opened his heart again in Psalm 103 to express what

he knew about the way God's heart worked. He spoke, "The LORD is merciful and gracious, slow to anger, and abounding in mercy.... He has not dealt with us according to our sins, nor punished us according to our iniquities" (Ps. 103:8, 10). He was saying, "When I deserve to be punished, He forgives me and restores me in love." He testified, "For as the heavens are high above the earth, so great is His mercy toward those who fear Him" (v. 11). David knew that God had removed his sins as far as the east is from the west.

> As a father has compassion on his children, so the LORD has compassion on those who fear him; for he knows how we are formed, he remembers that we are dust.
>
> —PSALM 103:13–14, NIV

This was David's revelation of God's heart. He learned to relate to God on the basis of God's passion for him rather than his own performance. He operated from an entirely different ground of confidence than most believers do. Beloved, only a student of God's emotions can recover so quickly after grievous compromise. Later David would write, "If You, LORD, should mark iniquities, O Lord, who could stand? But there is forgiveness with You, that You may be feared" (Ps. 130:3–4). God forgives us today so we will grow in the fear of God tomorrow. If He wiped us out today, we would never become mature, God-fearing people. This is God's strategy toward us. He wants to deal gently with us even though it requires burning our Ziklags. He does not

HE LEARNED TO RELATE TO GOD ON THE BASIS OF GOD'S PASSION FOR HIM RATHER THAN HIS OWN PERFORMANCE.

want to mark our iniquities but to forgive them so we can go on to be great in love.

Our confidence never needs to be based on the last month or week or year, or whether we had a season of victory or failure. He wants our confidence to be based in the revelation of His desire for us and His work on the cross. This is the confidence of true worshipers.

Confidence in God's love is a rare thing on the earth. John tells us perfect love casts out fear (1 John 4:18). This also means casting unholy fear, or condemnation, out of our relationship with God. This will be absolutely necessary if we are to make it through those unprecedented troubles of the last days. Many of us need to overcome a spirit of fear that gets in the way of our intimacy with God. We will see how to do that in the next chapter.

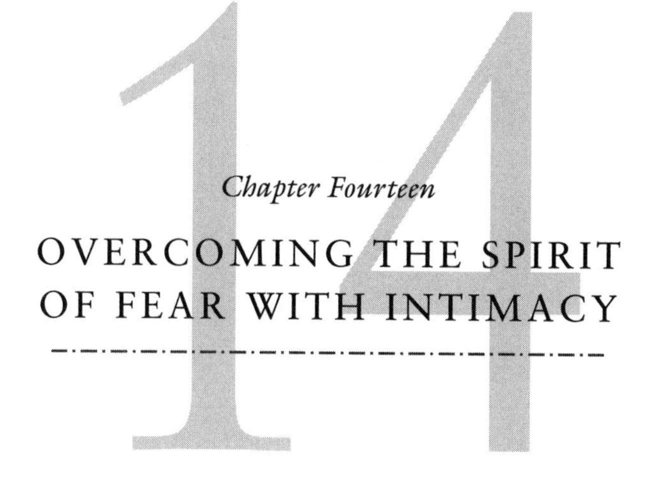

Chapter Fourteen

OVERCOMING THE SPIRIT OF FEAR WITH INTIMACY

In the wilderness of Judea, just after John baptized Jesus at the Jordan River, the heavens opened and the voice of the Lord broke forth. As Jesus came up out of the water, the Spirit of God descended on Him like a dove, and His Father leaned over the balcony of heaven to say, "This is My beloved Son, in whom I am well pleased" (Matt. 3:17). With this thunderous statement, the Father prepared His Son's heart to enter into one of the great tests of His earthly life—the temptation of Satan in the wilderness.

Scripture records only three occasions when God the Father spoke to Jesus audibly. This was one of them. It is highly significant to us that just before Jesus encountered Satan personally in Matthew 4, the Father renewed the sense of connection and intimacy between Father and Son. Though Jesus is fully God, in His humanity He needed refreshing. He was not automatically strengthened, but, like us, He grew physically and mentally weary. And so this is a pattern for how God the Father deals with us. As

Jesus faced the daunting task ahead of Him in the wilderness, the voice of His Father reassured Him of the greatest privilege given the human race: that we can enjoy intimacy with the Godhead. This intimacy empowered Jesus to face the trials of the enemy, and this same intimacy equips us to overcome the trials of life. Indeed, this assurance of our special closeness to God is the only thing that can equip and prepare our hearts for this crucial hour in history, when great revival and the greatest divine judgments are about to break forth. I'm convinced that just as the Father spoke strength to Jesus by expressing His delight in Him, so God will empower us by assuring us of His delight in us. Nothing else will be able to sustain our hearts.

In the final hours of human history, darkness and light will increase simultaneously. Men's hearts will faint for fear (Luke 21:26). Incredible revival will proceed parallel to the horrors of increasing sin. Satan's rage and God's judgments will crescendo side by side. As the kingdom of darkness grows stronger, the kingdom of God will grow abundantly strong. The gray area of indecision will be removed as believers and unbelievers alike will decide if they are passionate for Jesus or passionate against Him. Jesus said:

> But when you see Jerusalem surrounded by armies, then know that its desolation is near. Then let those who are in Judea flee to the mountains.... For these are the days of vengeance, that all things which are written may be fulfilled.... For there will be great distress in the land and wrath upon this people. And they will fall by the edge of the sword, and be led away captive into all nations. And Jerusalem will be trampled by Gentiles until the times of the Gentiles are fulfilled. And there will be signs in the sun, in the moon, and in the stars; and on the earth distress of nations, with perplexity, the sea and the waves roaring; men's hearts failing them from fear and the expectation of those things which are

> coming on the earth, for the powers of heaven will be shaken. Then they will see the Son of Man coming in a cloud with power and great glory. Now when these things begin to happen, look up and lift up your heads, because your redemption draws near.
>
> —LUKE 21:20–28

In this stunning prophesy, Jesus described a tremendous drama of divine judgment and demonic activity taking place simultaneously. He prophesied two distinct time frames. First, the national trauma in A.D. 70, which was to take place forty years after the His death. The Roman army would annihilate Jerusalem and bring tremendous destruction on the nation of Israel. Second, He spoke of global trauma at the end of the age that would parallel the great trouble of A.D. 70 but would far surpass it. Jesus said it would be the most terrible time in all human history.

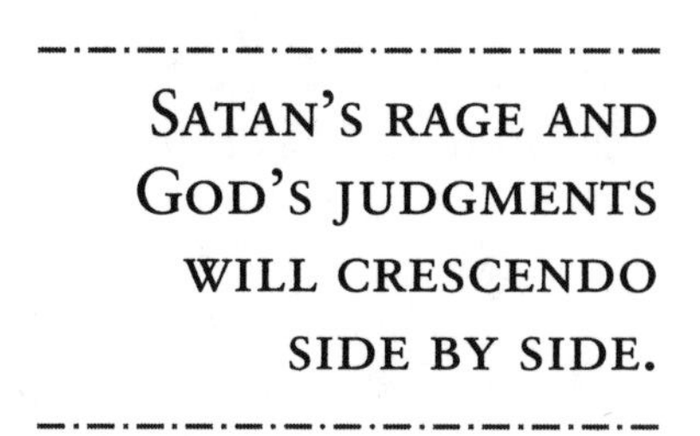

> For then there will be great tribulation, such as has not been since the beginning of the world until this time, no, nor ever shall be. And unless those days were shortened, no flesh would be saved; but for the elect's sake those days will be shortened.
>
> —MATTHEW 24:21–22

I want to draw our attention to the words in the prophecy from Luke 21, where Jesus said that men's hearts would fail them because of fear (v. 26). Fear and panic are going to increase, not decrease, as the years go by. They will dominate the human race in the last generation and will become one of the great sources of torment used by the enemy. He will vex believers and unbelievers alike as we march toward the Second Coming of Christ. In that day, overcoming fear will be one of the foremost issues the body of Christ will take on. The Lord will anoint us with answers to comfort fainting or failing hearts.

How to Be Delivered From Fear

What is the path to overcoming great fear in the End Times? The examples of Jesus and David make it clear: they overcame fear by seeking God's face in intimacy. They did what we have been studying throughout this book and gazed upon the heart of God, encountering His beauty. David wrote:

> One thing I have desired of the LORD, that will I seek: that I may dwell in the house of the LORD all the days of my life, to behold the beauty of the LORD, and to inquire in His temple. For in the time of trouble He shall hide me in His pavilion; in the secret place of His tabernacle He shall hide me.... And now my head shall be lifted up above my enemies all around me.... Hear, O LORD, when I cry with my voice! Have mercy also upon me, and answer me. When You said, "Seek My face," my heart said to You, "Your face, LORD, I will seek."
>
> —PSALM 27:4–8

The *trouble* David talked about was manifold, but mainly it was the trouble of people seeking to harm him. This is one of the worst kinds of trouble, as you may be able to attest. It is awful to walk around with that sinking feeling in your stomach because somebody at work, church, your neighborhood, or school is out to get you. You want to repair the situation, but often you can't, so you learn to live with the reality of having an enemy, as David did. He practically walked around with a big target on him from the day Saul rejected him. Later in life, people in his own court, his closest friends and advisors, wanted him dead. But he proclaimed that God would hide him in His shelter. His words shine a big light on the answer of how to carry our hearts in the hour of persecution and great trouble that comes from evil people.

> The LORD is my light and my salvation; whom shall I fear? The LORD is the strength of my life; of whom shall I be afraid? When the wicked came against me to eat up my flesh... they stumbled and fell. Though an army may encamp against me, my heart shall not fear; though war may rise against me, in this I will be confident.
>
> —PSALM 27:1–3

The first claim David made was, "The Lord is my light." With these words, he declared that the Lord would help him with the spirit of revelation. One of the privileges God has given the church is access to divine information. We receive it in a general sense through His Word, which makes our hearts strong for the days ahead. Many believers don't study enough the powerful information freely offered in the Word. This is God's number-one way of equipping us for the coming pressures. In the Bible, God reveals His plan for the End Times and for eternity, everything we can expect to happen to us as believers. But He also gives us divine information in a more personal and specific way through the prophetic anointing, which David referred to here. I along with many others believe that the Lord is now raising up and releasing the prophetic ministry in the church all over the earth on a scale nobody has yet seen.

THE EXAMPLES OF JESUS AND DAVID MAKE IT CLEAR: THEY OVERCAME FEAR BY SEEKING GOD'S FACE IN INTIMACY.

> And it shall come to pass in the last days, says God, that I will pour out of My Spirit on all flesh; your sons and your daughters shall prophesy, your young men shall see visions, your old men shall dream dreams.
>
> —Acts 2:17

God will surely give us information about things just around the corner, divine revelation through dreams and visions. This will be common in the End-Times church. Paul testified of having divine light in a time of fear. When he was about to enter the city of Corinth, he was afraid, but then the Lord appeared to him and bolstered his courage to enter the city. The Lord said to him, "Do not be afraid, but speak, and do not keep silent; for I am with you, and no one will attack you to hurt you; for I have many people in the city" (Acts 18:9–10). This information had a tremendous impact on Paul's heart. Fear was seemingly getting a hold on him, but God gave him victory by visiting him in a vision. I imagine Paul saying to himself afterward, "Whew, that really makes a difference. I'm not afraid anymore." David and many other men and women of the Bible received divine information about their lives and futures. We can get the same kind of insight about calamities and God's protection for us in the days to come. This divine information is available because of our intimacy with Him.

> YOU WON'T GET A FAT BOOK OF PERSONAL HISTORY WITH HIM UNLESS YOU LEAVE THE SAFE ZONE.

Your Personal History With God

The second truth that empowered David to overcome fear through intimacy with God was, "The Lord is my salvation." He came to this conclusion by drawing from his personal history in

God. He remembered the times God had delivered him with power. He was testifying that the Lord is the God of the breakthrough, and He will break into our circumstances with power to save. In this verse, David did not mean salvation from hell, but salvation from a crisis or dilemma. He was referring to miraculous intervention. This truth will uphold our hearts when sin ensnares us and during the crises at the end of the age. We will draw on our history in Him, recalling that He is a God who has granted us deliverance many times in the past from external and internal struggles.

Each believer has a personal history in God that has been developed through the years. It may be lengthy or it may be thin, but the Lord wants to give each of us as individuals a substantial private history so we can write our own faith book, so to speak. The breakthroughs of God in our lives come intermittently, one here and one there, yet over time they add up, and we start to build a significant private history in God. David's history in God was constantly growing. Each time he stepped out of fear and into the strength and boldness of God, a new page was added to his personal faith book.

How do we gain history in God? By getting out of the boat as Peter did to walk on the water. We break out of our area of ease. Many times in my own life I have been up against the wall with no time left on the clock. Then, suddenly, God broke in with a surprise answer. I love it when that happens. Time and again, He answers me, and I experience His breakthrough in the nick of time. He often allows me to go right to the edge. Some years ago, in the midst of serious pressure, before the answer suddenly came, I looked up at the Lord and said, "You're waiting until the last minute on purpose!" I imagine He winked at me and said, "You got it. Then you will know I heard you all along."

You won't get a fat book of personal history with Him unless you leave the safe zone. The Lord wants us to sow financially into the kingdom of God so we can experience economic breakthroughs. He wants us to lay our hands on the sick so we can discover His power in healing even though at times nothing appears to happen. When we are in difficulty, He wants us to press in and seek Him for a breakthrough. David overcame fear by recalling his personal history, remembering the breakthroughs of God in times past. He gave us a general statement: "When the wicked came against me to eat up my flesh, my enemies and my foes, they stumbled and fell" (Ps. 27:2). He was saying they stumbled because the God of heaven broke in. It looked like sure defeat for him. Then the Lord came swiftly to his aid, and David was stunned with gratitude. Fear disappeared. When the dark night comes and we face the great troubles prophesied in Luke 21, we will draw upon our private history in God. Why should our hearts faint for fear like the unbelievers? We will overcome fear through a personal history in His faithfulness. We should agree with David's testimony and say, "I will not be afraid because I remember that God has continually been my salvation and deliverer."

FEAR WILL NOT GO AWAY BY ITSELF; WE HAVE TO RISE UP AND RESIST IT.

"The Lord is the strength of my life"

David also said, "The LORD is the strength of my life" (Ps. 27:1), testifying that God was his emotional strength, the strength of his heart. This is another facet of our intimacy with Him, which shields us from fear. Beloved, there is an emotional strength offered us by God. Paul prayed that divine might would touch our inner man, that our emotions would be made strong: "That He would grant you . . . to be strengthened with might through His Spirit in your inner man" (Eph. 3:16). He was referring to our emotional being.

God surely will supernaturally strengthen our inner man with divine might during the time of crisis and risk, when the healing is delayed, when the finances are gone, and when the persecution continues. He fills our souls with strength that we might stand in confidence. This is a supernatural gift and an anointing on the inside of us that enables us to keep going though it appears we have every reason to quit. Not quitting is itself an act of God's grace within us. But He will do more than that: He will cause your heart, your emotions to become buoyant and powerful, to be alive in God. Twice in Psalm 27, David asks, "Of whom shall I be afraid?" I love the jaunty confidence of that statement. When the Lord delivers us from fear, it doesn't mean we will never feel fear again, but that it's no longer a predominant reality in our life. Fear is no longer our preoccupation. It becomes something the enemy unsuccessfully tempts us with, a sideshow of his failure.

"Though an army encamps against me, I shall not fear"

Fear will not go away by itself; we have to rise up and resist it. To uplift his heart and overcome the darkness of fear, David prophesied, "Though an army may encamp against me, my heart shall not fear; though war may rise against me, in this I will be confident" (Ps. 27:3). David decided that whenever his heart started wavering, he would move into a place of communion with God instead of caving under the weight of the attack. We must do our part of the division of labor when fear comes. We are not to just endure it. We must arise in confidence and assert the opposite of what fear is telling us.

As you read the Book of Psalms, you see a progression of maturity in David's life toward fear. He didn't always brim with confidence in the face of it. When David was in his twenties, fear (and Saul's army) chased him from cave to cave. When he was about twenty-eight years old, fear overcame him in a grievous way in Ziklag (1 Sam. 27). My guess is that he wrote Psalm 13 in the wake of that period. But if you skip ahead to Psalm 27, you see a different sort of man: confident in victory, scoffing at fear, bold in the Lord. David was in his forties when he wrote Psalm 27; he had been king for some years. He had experience and intimacy with God. On our journey to the fearlessness of Psalm 27, we too have to go through the struggle of faith described in Psalm 13. We can't leapfrog Psalm 13 on our way to victory. That psalm says:

> How long, O LORD? Will You forget me forever? How long will You hide Your face from me? How long shall I take counsel in my soul, having sorrow in my heart daily? How long will my enemy be exalted over me? Consider and hear me, O LORD my God; enlighten my eyes, lest I sleep the sleep of death; lest my enemy say, "I have prevailed against him"; lest those who trouble me rejoice when I am moved. But I have trusted in Your mercy; my heart shall rejoice in Your salvation. I will sing to the Lord, because He has dealt bountifully with me.

We have examined David's heart during those months in Ziklag—how the promises seemed a million miles away; how King Saul was exalting over David; how even David's sins conspired against him. David was a portrait of a man overcome with anxiety. But then he cried out with desperation, "Consider and hear me, O LORD my God; enlighten my eyes." He cried in essence, "Let me see divine information, and my soul shall live! Give me light!" In Psalm 27 David said, "I have light!" But in Psalm 13, he said, "I can't figure anything out! Saul is winning, my own heart is yielding to fear, and I am compromising. Give me understanding, or I will sleep the sleep of death. I am filled with sorrow." In confusion, he cried, "Lest my enemy say, 'I have prevailed against him'; lest those who trouble me rejoice when I am moved" (Ps. 13:4). He was saying, "God! Don't let the enemy win! I want to move into my calling! I want to move into a free heart!"

Suddenly, a burst of faith bloomed in David's spirit.

> But I have trusted in Your mercy; my heart shall rejoice in Your salvation. I will sing to the LORD, because He has dealt bountifully with me.
>
> —PSALM 13:5–6

David fought the fight of faith by exercising his heart through song. In this season, his song was not the faithful, irrepressible one he wrote in later days. It was a song that rode the pendulum back and forth from "I'm going to lose!" to "I'm going to win!" He sounded a little schizophrenic. Yet even in confusion, he pressed in. He knew that God's answer would come as he wrestled with the truth of God in his own soul. He kept rebounding to the place of prayer. Finally, that rebounding yielded results.

> One thing I have desired of the LORD, that will I seek: that I may dwell in the house of the LORD all the days of my life, to behold the beauty of the LORD, and to inquire in His temple.
>
> —PSALM 27:4

This verse tells the entire story of David's journey. He confronted fear by throwing himself into intimacy with God. He pressed into revelation about God's beauty. He knew that his safety was in living with a fascinated heart that transformed his inner life. We too experience victory in the midst of the struggle as we seek intimacy with God.

> For in the time of trouble He shall hide me in His pavilion; in the secret place of His tabernacle He shall hide me; He shall set me high upon a rock. And now

> my head shall be lifted up above my enemies all around me; therefore I will offer sacrifices of joy in His tabernacle; I will sing, yes, I will sing praises to the LORD.
>
> —PSALM 27:5–6

The breakthrough anointing over fear is found in the secret place of God's beauty. Fear does not dominate the heart there because a superior pleasure upholds the heart. It is a lifestyle of encounter and intimacy with the beauty of God that rescues us from fear. This was a drastically new concept when David put it forth. Moses, who lived five hundred years earlier, popularized the teaching that you cannot see the face of God and live. In Exodus 20:19, the people said, "If we even hear God's voice we will die." David answered that paradigm of God with his own experience, which created a vastly different paradigm: "God Most High told me that He wanted to show me His face." This is the first time God ever said to the human race that He desired us to seek His face. David was the first person to declare this. His new teaching was that the God of heaven does not want to strike us dead when He shows us His face, but He desires to bring us into the experience of closeness and comfort with Him.

When you consider the lack of intimacy with Jesus in the present-day church, it is no surprise that believers and unbelievers are tormented by fear nearly to the same degree. Fear is not sufficiently driven away by confession of God's Word alone, although I believe in that. We must confess God's Word and the specific prophetic decrees He has given us. We need to stick to our confession in the midst of the enemy's assault. When all is said and done, the spirit of fear is best driven out by a spirit of intimacy. And in this we must persevere.

> I would have lost heart, unless I had believed that I would see the goodness of the LORD in the land of the

> living. Wait on the LORD; be of good courage, and He shall strengthen your heart; wait, I say, on the LORD!
>
> —PSALM 27:13–14

David would have lost all hope if he hadn't known that sooner of later he would experience a breakthrough of God's goodness. God usually hides the breakthrough until it comes. We can't always see it coming. Then *bam*! It hits. Until then we have to aggressively press in to see God's beauty. David put it this way: "Wait on the LORD; be of good courage, and He shall strengthen your heart!" We don't wilt on the side of the road. Rather, we pray courageously, seek His face diligently, and stand firm with what we know to be true. Our souls will be anchored in the unchanging, unyielding love of God. We will experience the promise Jesus made to His disciples: "I am with you always, even to the end of the age" (Matt. 28:20). This promise is for intimacy and nearness. It will sustain our hearts.

WE TOO EXPERIENCE VICTORY IN THE MIDST OF THE STRUGGLE AS WE SEEK INTIMACY WITH GOD.

We have been looking at important aspects of David's journey as a man who went through seasons of preparation, who ran to God instead of away from Him during his compromise, and who overcame fear with intimacy. Now we turn to one of the most exciting realities of David's life that is being reawakened in the church today.

15

Chapter Fifteen

CONSUMED WITH ZEAL FOR NIGHT-AND-DAY PRAYER

In this generation, I believe the Lord is calling young and old, rich and poor to the ministry of night-and-day prayer and worship as He did in the days of David. Many scriptures from Genesis to Revelation make it clear that God has scheduled a prayer movement to sweep the entire planet in the generation in which the Lord returns. Scripture also seems to indicate that there will be a great harvest of souls at the same time. More than a billion souls will come into the kingdom. These new believers won't enter a spiritual vacuum where their initial exuberance is ground down to business as usual. They will enter a spiritual atmosphere that has been revolutionized by night-and-day prayer. I am convinced we are at the beginning of the generation that will reach the pinnacle of worship and prayer ministry described in the Word of God. That means we have a lot to learn from David, who was a glorious prophetic picture of the End-Time house of prayer God will establish across the earth. David was a prophetic down payment and a token to encourage us today, and we should carefully study his example and the example of other zealous men in the Old Testament.

Even now you can observe what is happening in the body of Christ. A worship and prayer movement is rising up, birthed and orchestrated by the Holy Spirit, used by God to unify the church across cities and nations. It seems to have begun in the early 1980s or late 1970s, but it has been accelerating in the last five or ten years. Observers have watched in awe at the increase of prayer activity across the world in the last few decades. That increase will continue because it is following a divine pattern God is establishing from heaven. He is creating a worldwide prayer movement to prepare the church for the great harvest. As a result, thousands and thousands of men and women will be consumed with the zeal of God for His house.

A Perfect Portrait of Zeal

What does it mean to be consumed by zeal? It's best to see it demonstrated in real life, and for a truly awesome picture, we should focus on one of the greatest leaders of the Old Testament, a man who is often overlooked. If we are to stay on course in our generation, we must learn from the experience of zealous people of the past, and this man is one of the most zealous we find in Scripture.

In 586 B.C., Nebuchadnezzar and the Babylonian army wiped out Jerusalem and took the Israelites into slavery. The temple in Jerusalem was burned to the ground. The prophets Jeremiah, Ezekiel, and Daniel witnessed it firsthand. It was the darkest hour the nation had experienced to that point in their history. But after seventy years, about fifty thousand Israelites were released from captivity, and they left Babylon and walked back to Israel, a hike that took about five months and covered around seven hundred miles. They rebuilt the temple, or the house of prayer as it was called, and during times of discouragement God was faithful to break in with power and strengthen them until the temple was completed.

A generation later, about 444 B.C., Nehemiah, an incredible apostolic figure, called with great zeal for the people to build walls around the city. He was intense and tough, which is exactly what the survivors of the Babylonian captivity needed. They were in distress and reproach, and the wall of Jerusalem was broken down and its gates burned (Neh. 1:3). Walls would protect the temple, the house of prayer, so night-and-day prayers would rise before God. Nehemiah saw what was at stake, so he called on the people to build the walls so they would no longer bear reproach (Neh. 2:17). His zeal resonated with the people, and they rose to the occasion (v. 18). What a day that was! After building the walls of protection, singers and musicians began night-and-day ministry of worshiping before the Lord. With the protective walls in place, they spent the next twelve years with the house of prayer in full swing and the people learning how to move into intimacy with God's heart.

A WORSHIP AND PRAYER MOVEMENT IS RISING UP, BIRTHED AND ORCHESTRATED BY THE HOLY SPIRIT, USED BY GOD TO UNIFY THE CHURCH ACROSS CITIES AND NATIONS.

But Nehemiah had to return to Susa, the capital of Persia, and was absent for several years (Neh. 13:6). While he was away, the people's zeal slumped, and they fell into negligence and passivity. Enthusiasm for the house of prayer faded away. When Nehemiah returned to Jerusalem five or ten years later, he was brokenhearted at what he saw (v. 8). The singers and Levites had given up singing and quit the prayer meetings. The people had stopped giving money and had fired the priests and singers. They apparently concluded that it was all a bit fanatical; after all, the business of getting their military and government established was much more important than doing some weird worship thing at the house of prayer. They had to think logically, practically. But Nehemiah contended with the rulers and cried, "Why is the house of God forsaken?" (v. 11). He pleaded with them to remember how God had delivered them from Babylon. With godly vigor, he gathered the priests together and set the musicians and singers back in their places. Nehemiah's heart reverberated with God's own zeal. He was consumed by it as he faced the task of protecting God's house night and day.

That is exactly the kind of zeal we must have today about the house of prayer. David said it best. "Great is the LORD, and greatly to be praised; His greatness is unsearchable" (Ps. 145:3). This is one of the most important statements David ever made, and he made it four times in the Book of Psalms (Ps. 48:1; 96:4; 145:3; 147:5). David saw that God's greatness is unrestrainable, unexplainable, uncontainable, and beyond our capacity to grasp. Day and night the seraphim cry out, "Holy, holy, holy, Lord God Almighty, who was and is and is to come!" (Rev. 4:8). Their continual testimony gives witness to the unsearchable nature of God's greatness and inexhaustible beauty. That was David's motivation in establishing the house of prayer in his day. After drinking from the ocean of God's emotions and affections, he lifted his voice to say, "I tell you, He is great, and He must be praised!"

God's greatness and beauty is the sustaining foundation of all houses of prayer, from far back in the Old Testament to our present day. God's greatness demands a response, and we respond by personally and corporately praising Him. As we give ourselves to our obsession with His greatness, we become consumed with making sure He is greatly praised on the earth by fiery, abandoned, lovesick people.

This deep conviction has been burning in my spirit for some time. It is in my heart to see a *habitation* of God in my city of Kansas City, Missouri. My heart has said to the Lord that I am going to labor at building His house until we see a place of God's dwelling built there. But I'm not the only one with this vision. God has stirred many others around the world with this same urgency. He wants believers across the earth to take hold of the dream of worshiping the great God with abandonment and with skillful singers and musicians. He wants to impart the vision for continuous praise in cities everywhere. Is there not cause to lift up His praise night and day? Is it not something to live for—building a habitation of God on the earth?

We Are Zealous Because God Is Zealous

Our zeal comes from the nature and personality of God Himself. In the five- to ten-year gap while Nehemiah was away, God anointed Malachi to prophesy to the Israelites. Through his words we see God motivating His people to build His house in the midst of discouragement. He began with, "'I have loved you,' says the LORD" (Mal. 1:2). Notice that in the generation God was rebuilding the house of prayer, He began with the message of His affection and love. He affirmed them by saying, "I love you. I really do." He promised they would delight in Him (Mal. 3:1).

> DAVID SAW THAT GOD'S GREATNESS IS UNRESTRAINABLE, UNEXPLAINABLE, AND BEYOND OUR CAPACITY TO GRASP.

Malachi spoke to leaders who in spite of their leadership were not on fire for God. They had answered the call of God and actually began to do the labors in the house of God. They said *yes* to the prophetic history and believed in the prophetic words. But when it came down to the substance of their hearts, they were neither lovesick nor fascinated nor zealous for God. They had no consuming passion to make His name great. To bring them into right motivation, the Lord beckoned them with His own love. He was not trying to build a new ministry organization called the House of Prayer so He could feel better about Himself because people were praising Him all the time; rather, He was kick-starting a love exchange between heaven and earth.

The prophet Zechariah brought the same message. "Thus says the LORD of hosts: 'I am zealous...for Zion with great zeal'" (Zech. 1:14). The message was that His heart was burning with desire. The revelation of God's desire and affection is the foundation for building His house. He wants builders consumed with "one thing" of extravagant love and devotion. He wants worshipers after His own heart. Jesus displayed zeal for His house when He walked through the temple with a whip, overturning the money tables and driving out the animals (John 2:17). He manifested the same zeal that David spoke of when he said, "Zeal for Your house has eaten me up" (Ps. 69:9). God's zeal springs from love. The Lord calls us to build the house of prayer because the house of prayer is all about Him and catching the waves of divine affection from God's heart. The prayer movement at the end of the age is called love. It is about love for God, love for one another, and love for the lost.

> I am zealous for Zion with great zeal; with great fervor I am zealous for her.
>
> —ZECHARIAH 8:2

Oh, the zeal of God! The word *fervor* literally means heat or rage. God portrays His zeal as something hot within Him, an unrestrained desire, a burning passion. His zeal is a powerful and positive aspect of His heart, not something to be afraid of. God possesses intimate knowledge and deep concern about every individual in His kingdom. He has deep, deep feelings of emotion about His people. He is not in the least bit distant or aloof. Even when the enemy tries to convince me that the Lord is not full of zeal or love, and I find myself saying, "Lord, am I on the back burner? Did You forget about me?" the answer is *no*. The Lord burns with heat, rage, and intense desire for all believers, including you and me.

I saw a Bill Gates biography the other day, and the commentator said that for fifteen years he would go to bed at 2 A.M. and get up at 6 A.M. He was fanatical to see a career breakthrough. I was proud to realize I know believers who have as much zeal as Bill Gates does, but they have it for an imperishable crown. I am not saying you need to sleep four hours a night. But we should have zeal for our cause in history. I'm not waiting for this type of ministry to be popular. I'm not catching a new trend. I don't care if it's ever popular. I have sunk the boats and burned the bridges behind me. I am going for it, and I am looking for a few men and women—I don't care if they're fifteen years old or ninety—who say, "I'm not waiting for the famous guys to do it. I'm not waiting for the best-selling book to come out. I'm going for it!"

THE PRAYER MOVEMENT AT THE END OF THE AGE IS CALLED LOVE. IT IS ABOUT LOVE FOR GOD, LOVE FOR ONE ANOTHER, AND LOVE FOR THE LOST.

I have heard many friends over the years say, "I want to have balance in my ministry." I tell them, "I believe in Jesus' version of balance, and He was not considered balanced by anyone in His day. Even the apostles did not think that He was balanced. If balance means retreating into risk-free leadership with no power, I'm not interested in balance. It won't deliver anyone."

Others have told me, "I'm interested in compassion ministry. We have to water the hard stuff down to get people to come." But if you want to show compassion to a little boy who's demonized or has a terminal disease, you don't play patty-cake with the problem. You cast that devil out and give the boy his life back.

We have to be filled with the zeal of God. One of the primary ways God displays His zeal is by rebuilding the place of worship. In Zechariah 1:16, He stated this purpose in His heart. "I am returning to Jerusalem with mercy; My house shall be built in it." With zeal and mercy, He will build the house of worship and prayer in Jerusalem and all over the earth. Beloved, we are recipients of God's zeal and mercy. He has great zeal that His people would cultivate grace to live a life of prayer. The Lord will lead His church into prayer in a dozen different ways, and all are valid. People will give themselves to lives of prayer for numerous reasons, but at the very core of it all is a God raging with zealous desire. We desire Him because He desires us. We are zealous because He is zealous. When we encounter that emotion, it translates into renewed energy to give ourselves to prayer, fasting, the prophetic ministry, and the End-Time harvest.

Gripped With Zeal for God's House

David knew that the fullness of God would not come to pass in his generation without night-and-day prayer, which is why he was consumed with zeal for the house of God. This vision so consumed him that he set up a prophetic worship ministry to the Lord with four thousand musicians and two hundred eighty-eight singers (1 Chron. 23–25). One of the central themes of Scripture ever since that time is how God has been building the house of prayer throughout the generations. There is struggle in the process of fulfilling God's purpose. Through the Word we see how He gathers the people, they fall and stumble in the process, then He gathers again them and gives them victory. He allows struggle so that when the victory comes, our hearts are protected by the grace of humility. At the end of natural history, God says, "My house shall be called a house of prayer for all nations" (Isa. 56:7).

It is very important to understand that God named the temple "the house of prayer." The building of the temple was essentially and mostly about worship and prayer. Five hundred years later, after the temple was built, Jesus came along and confirmed that God called the temple a house of prayer (Matt. 21:13). In all of our studies of the temple, we must understand it is the house of prayer, a place of love, worship, and encounter, not just a historic temple with religious rituals attached to it. It's about a worldwide church living in a spirit of prayer with fasting and overcome with His love so that the events at the end of the age will be released.

PEOPLE WILL GIVE THEMSELVES TO LIVES OF PRAYER FOR NUMEROUS REASONS, BUT AT THE VERY CORE OF IT ALL IS A GOD RAGING WITH ZEALOUS DESIRE.

David caught wind of this passion in God's heart and refused to give himself to anything else until he saw it come to pass in his day. But his decision brought much affliction.

> LORD, remember David and all his afflictions; how he swore to the LORD, and vowed to the Mighty One of Jacob: "Surely I will not go into the chamber of my house, or go up to the comfort of my bed; I will not give sleep to my eyes or slumber to my eyelids, until I

> find a place for the LORD, a dwelling place for the Mighty One of Jacob."
>
> —PSALM 132:1–5

When we give ourselves to building the house of prayer, we will meet God in affliction. Affliction is a part of the divine equation, as we learned earlier from the apostle Paul and the prophet Daniel. There are two different godly responses to affliction found in Scripture. In some of the affliction we rise up in the name of Jesus and drive it out; other affliction we endure as our love grows and matures. In Psalm 132, the psalmist prayed that the Lord would remember all that David went through. Elsewhere, David said, "Indeed I have taken much trouble to prepare for the house of the LORD" (1 Chron. 22:14). He spent his money, time, and strength on this preoccupation and pressed on through many types of affliction. Even his own sin didn't hold him back. The cry of his heart to the Lord was, "You will be greatly praised!" Everything in his life became subservient to that zeal for God's dwelling place that "ate him up."

> YOU HAVE BEEN BROUGHT TO THE KINGDOM FOR SUCH A TIME AS THIS. GOD IS RAISING UP PEOPLE IN THIS GENERATION WHO RESPOND TO GOD AS DAVID DID.

God is raising up a company of people all over the earth with this kind of zeal. They burn within for this moment and this purpose in history. They won't find their value in their pet ministry ideas or personal fulfillment, but in building a dwelling place of God.

The End-Time Prayer and Worship Movement

Jesus said that when night-and-day prayer is in place, speedy justice will be released in the cities of the earth (Luke 18:8). Speedy justice speaks of unprecedented revival with signs and wonders. Throughout the Word of God, we find only one thing that ultimately stops the power of darkness at the end of the age. It is the prayer and worship movement within the church worldwide. *This is not optional to God.* He requires it to bring this age to fruition. It is an invitation with urgency. It's not enough to read and agree; we must jump in with all our hearts and find how we can be part of this global movement.

Our twenty-four-hour ministry in Kansas City is a small prayer ministry. We are not the house of prayer in Kansas City, but one of many catalysts for prayer. We understand that the house of prayer is not one or two churches' little ministry idea, but the core identity of the church worldwide in this age and in the age to come. One prayer ministry at one church cannot contain or express it. Even a whole city full of prayer cannot express it. All local houses of prayer are merely catalysts pushing us to the time when the whole church operates in the anointing of intimacy and authority to speak on the earth and see the heavens move at the sound of their words.

Beloved, that is the glorious hour in which we live. You have been brought to the kingdom for such a time as this. God is raising up people in this generation who respond to God as David did, becoming students of His emotions, seeing God for who He really is with the strong passion and love for us in His heart. That transforms us and puts us on a path to realizing our earthly destiny. We are empowered by happy holiness; we become people of one thing, men and women after God's own heart. We feel what He feels and love what He loves, and that compels us to contend for the full expression of the apostolic faith in our day. We acquire

God's own zeal to create a habitation for Him in the earth, and so we commit ourselves to being part of the prayer movement being raised up by the Holy Spirit. We will have the pleasure of seeing the largest amount of people in history come into the kingdom at the deepest level of love. We will witness the most powerful revival the world has ever seen. And when the age draws to a close, we will lift our voices as the bride in unity with the Holy Spirit and cry, "Come, Lord Jesus," until He splits the sky and we are caught up together with Him forever!

Do you want more
After God's Own Heart?
For a **free** *After God's Own Heart* study guide,
register online at www.fotb.com/agoh.

ABOUT THE AUTHOR

Mike Bickle leads the Friends of the Bridegroom Missions Base (www.fotb.com) and the International House of Prayer of Kansas City (IHOP-KC), which has continued in nonstop prayer with worship and fasting teams for 24 hours a day, 365 days a year, for over four years. IHOP-KC currently has over 400 full-time staff who serve the Lord in intercession, worship, and fasting as they are being equipped to fulfill the Great Commission by reaching out in evangelism, prophetic ministry, healing the sick, and feeding the poor.

The Friends of the Bridegroom (FOTB) Missions Base

In John 3:29, John the Baptist described himself as a "friend of the Bridegroom." His identity and joy were found in being a voice that prepared his generation for the first coming of Jesus. Across the globe today, the Holy Spirit is drawing hearts into a movement of worship and prayer that will result in a host of individuals who, like John, will function as "friends of the bridegroom" going forth to fulfill the Great Commission and prepare the way of the Second Coming of Jesus.

Our missions base includes eight distinct ministries. Seven are focused on training and/or outreach. However, at the very center of all we do at the missions base is the 24-hour-a-day prayer furnace. We call this nonstop worship with prayer the International House of Prayer of Kansas City. It is at the core of all we do. The FOTB missions base in Kansas City is committed to prayer, fasting, and the Great Commission as we go forth in the forerunner spirit exemplified in the life of John the Baptist. IHOP-KC is currently staffed by 400 missionaries; each one raised their own support, and all have given their lives to wholehearted passion for Jesus Christ expressed in extravagant devotion. With weak hearts that are rooted and grounded in love, these missionaries ask the Lord to move upon hearts, change the atmosphere of the city, and turn the nations of the earth to the Son.

The other seven ministries flowing out of our missions base include: the Forerunner School of Ministry, Children's Equipping Center, Communications & Media Center, Shiloh Prophetic Ministries, the Israel Mandate, Apostolic Teams, and the International Missions Center.

What is the International House of Prayer?

On September 19, 1999, a prayer and worship meeting began in South Kansas City that continues this very hour. For over four years, night-and-day worship with intercession has gone up before the throne of God. Convinced that Jesus is worthy of incessant adoration, men and women of all ages from across the globe are giving themselves to extravagant love expressed through 24/7 prayer. Structured in eighty-four two-hour meetings a week, full teams of musicians, singers, and intercessors lift their voices in praise and supplication, asking God to fulfill His promise and give the nations of the earth to Jesus as His inheritance.

Why 24/7 worship and prayer?

Jesus said the harvest is plentiful, so His disciples should pray to the Lord of the harvest to send out laborers. Traditionally, the church throughout history has sent out missionaries to preach the gospel without first encountering the heart of God through a lifestyle of prayer with fasting. When our hearts deeply experience the love of God in the place of worship and intercession, we are strengthened and empowered to give ourselves to the labor of the work of the kingdom with greater diligence and authority. Ministries are arising all over the earth that literally offer supplication night and day before the Lord and function as catalysts for the entire church becoming a house of prayer (Isa. 56:7), causing the work of the harvest to go forth with power and effectiveness.

INTERNSHIPS AT THE INTERNATIONAL HOUSE OF PRAYER IN KANSAS CITY

A generation of lovesick worshipers...
An army of abandoned warriors...
Sending forerunners to the nations...

Three- to six-month programs offered for all ages and in five different languages

- "One Thing" Internship (ages 18–25)
- Fire in the Night (night watch internship for ages 18–30)
- Simeon Company (ages 50 and up)
- Summer Teen Internships
- Intro to IHOP-KC
- International Summer Programs (ages 25–50)—training programs of the FOTB missions base and IHOP-KC

Forerunner School of Ministry
An Accredited Full-Time Bible School in Kansas City

Passion for Jesus : The Forerunner Ministry :
Centrality of Scripture :
Community of Believers : 24/7 Intercessory Worship :
Evangelism and World Missions :
Ministry in the Power of the Spirit

Two- to Three-Year Study Programs
Committed to the Word of God and the Power of the Spirit

- Training worship leaders, preachers, pastors, evangelists, musicians, intercessors, and ambassadors in the marketplace

- Embracing the message of the forerunner
- Bible school of the FOTB missions base and IHOP-KC
- Full-time Bible school advancing the prayer, worship, and missions movement on the earth

www.fotb.com

OTHER RESOURCES BY MIKE BICKLE

PASSION FOR JESUS

The revelation of the passion and splendor of God's personality awakens fervent devotion to God and passion for Jesus. This book explores confidence in love birthed in the reality of loving and being loved by Him even in our weakness.

THE PLEASURES OF LOVING GOD

This book invites you on a most unique treasure hunt, a journey of discovery into intimacy with a Bridegroom God that loves, even likes you, and wants your friendship. Dimensions of the forerunner ministry and the house of prayer are also examined.

SONG OF SOLOMON AUDIO TEACHING

This completely revised and updated course on the Song of Songs is Mike's most comprehensive and powerful presentation on this glorious book to date. The CD version includes the study guide in PDF format.

SONG OF SOLOMON STUDY GUIDES (2 VOLUMES)

These study guides accompany the Song of Songs audio series. Packed with new material and fresh insight, this is Mike's most comprehensive and powerful presentation on this glorious book to date.

LIFE OF DAVID AUDIO TEACHING (2 VOLUMES, 10 TAPES EACH)

In this teaching series, Mike describes specific settings in David's life as recorded in 1 and 2 Samuel and relates them to the psalms that David wrote. Mike's main focus is the theme of God's beauty and how it empowers the believer's heart to be filled with extravagant love and worship.

For more information about resources from Mike Bickle and the International House of Prayer, or to request a free catalog, please call 1-800-552-2449 from 9 A.M. to 7 P.M. CST, Monday through Friday.

You can also visit our Web site and Web store at www.fotb.com.